The Theory and Practice of
GAMESMANSHIP

The Theory & Practice of

GAMESMANSHIP

or

THE ART OF WINNING GAMES
WITHOUT ACTUALLY
CHEATING

By

S T E P H E N   P O T T E R

ILLUSTRATED BY LT.-COL. FRANK WILSON

HENRY HOLT AND COMPANY
NEW YORK

TO
FRANCIS
MEYNELL

CONTENTS

vii

CONTENTS

LIST OF ILLUSTRATIONS

The Theory and Practice of
GAMESMANSHIP

Exterior of Lord Plummer's Fives-Court Adjoining " Hoses "

I

INTRODUCTORY

IF I HAVE been urged by my friends to take up my
pen, for once, to write of this subject—so difficult in
detail yet so simple in all its fundamental aspects—
I do so on one condition.   That I may be allowed to
say as strongly as possible that although my name has
been associated with this queer word " gamesmanship ", yet talk of priority in this kind of context is
almost meaningless.

It is true that in the twenties certain notes passed
between H. Farjeon and myself.   But equally notes
passed between H. Farjeon and F. Meynell.   It is
true that in March 1933 I conceived and wrote down
the word " gamesmanship " in a letter to Meynell.
Speaking of a forthcoming lawn tennis match against
two difficult opponents, I said " . . . we must employ
gamesmanship ".

It is true also that I was the most regular visitor—
" chairman " would imply a formality which

scarcely existed in those early days of argle-bargle and friendly disagreement—at the meetings which took place in pub parlour or empty billiard hall between G. Odoreida, Meynell, "Wayfarer" and myself. It is true that it was in these discussions that we evolved a basis of tactic and even plotted out a first rough field of stratagem which determined the *centres of development* from which the new technique spread in ever-widening circles. Small beginnings, indeed, for a movement which has spread so far from the confines of the country, and has shown itself too big to be contained by the World of Games for which it was fashioned.

But after the first formulation the spade-work was certainly done as much by Meynell and a few other devoted collaborators as by myself. And how well— wise after the event—we realise, now, from his practice and example, that Farjeon had the gist of the thing under his nose—the essential factors, the actions and reactions of the whole problem, without having the luck to see the patterning alignment, the overall theory, which made them make sense.

And yet had it not been for the dogged spade-work of Farjeon in the middle twenties, we should none of us now be enjoying the advantages of a theory which devolves as naturally from those meticulously collected data of his as Rutherford's enunciation of atomic structure derived from the experiments of that once obscure chemist Mierff.

Origins.

What is gamesmanship? Most difficult of questions to answer briefly. " The Art of Winning Games Without Actually Cheating "—that is my personal " working definition ". What is its object? There have been five hundred books written on the subject of games. Five hundred books on play and the tactics of play. Not one on the art of winning.

I well remember the gritty floor and the damp roller-towels of the changing-room where the idea of writing this book came to me. Yet my approach to the thing had been gradual.

There had been much that had puzzled me—I am speaking now of 1928—in the tension of our games of ping-pong at the Meynells'. Before that there had been the ardours and endurances of friendly lawn tennis at the Farjeons' house near Forest Hill, where Farjeon had wrought such havoc among so many visitors, by his careful construction of a " home court ", by the use he made of the net with the unilateral sag, or with a back line at the hawthorn end so nearly, yet not exactly, six inches wider than the back line at the sticky end. There had been a great deal of hard thinking on both sides during the wavering tide of battle, ending slightly in my favour, of the prolonged series of golf games between E. Lansbury and myself.

8th June 1931.

But it was in that changing-room after a certain game of lawn tennis in 1931 that the curtain was lifted, and I began to see. In those days I used to play lawn tennis for a small but progressive London College—Birkbeck, where I lectured. It happened that my partner at that time was C. Joad, the celebrated gamesman, who in his own sphere is known as metaphysician and educationist. Our opponents were usually young men from the larger colleges, competing against us not only with the advantage of age but also with a decisive advantage in style. They would throw the service ball very high in the modern manner: the back-hands, instead of being played from the navel, were played, in fact, on the back-hand, weight on right foot, in the exaggerated copy-book style of the time—a method of play which tends to reduce all games, as I believe, to a barrack-square drill by numbers; but, nevertheless, of acknowledged effectiveness.

In one match we found ourselves opposite a couple of particularly tall and athletic young men of this type from University College. We will call them Smith and Brown. The knock-up showed that, so far as play was concerned, Joad and I, playing for Birkbeck, had no chance. U. C. won the toss. It was Smith's service, and he cracked down a cannon-ball to Joad which moved so fast that Joad, while making some effort to suggest by his attitude that he had thought the ball was going to be a fault, nevertheless was unable to get near with his racket, which he did not even attempt to move. Score: fifteen-love. Service to me. I had had time to gauge the speed of this serve, and the next one did, in fact, graze the edge of my racket-frame. Thirty-love. Now Smith was serving again to Joad—who this time, as the ball came straight towards him, was able, by grasping the racket firmly with both hands, to receive the ball on the strings, whereupon the ball shot back to the other side and volleyed into the stop-netting near the ground behind Brown's feet.

Now here comes the moment on which not only this match, but so much of the future of British sport was to turn. Score: forty-love. Smith at S¹ (see Fig. 1) is about to cross over to serve to me (at P). When Smith gets to a point (K) *not less than one foot and not more than two feet* beyond the centre of the court (I know now what I only felt then—that timing is everything in this gambit), Joad (standing at J²) called across the net, in an even tone:

" Kindly say clearly, please, whether the ball was in or out."

Crude to our ears, perhaps. A Stone-Age implement. But beautifully accurate gamesmanship for 1931. For the student must realise that these two young men were both in the highest degree charming, well-mannered young men, perfect in their sportsmanship and behaviour. Smith (at point K) stopped dead.

SMITH: I'm so sorry—I *thought* it was out. (*The*

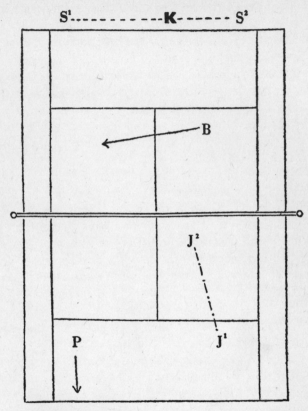

FIG. 1. *Key:*   P = Potter, J = Joad, S = Smith, B = Brown.
The dotted line represents Smith's path from S¹ to S². K represents the point he has reached on the cross-over when Joad has moved along the line (dot and dash) J¹ (where he had tried to return Smith's service) to J². Smith having arrived at, but not further than, the point K on the line S¹–S², J (Joad) speaks.

ball had hit the back netting twelve feet behind him before touching the ground.) But what did you think, Brown?

BROWN: I *thought* it was out—but do let's have it again.

JOAD: No, I don't want to have it again. I only want you to say clearly, if you will, whether the ball is in or out.

There is nothing more putting off to young university players than a slight suggestion that their etiquette or sportsmanship is in question. How well we know this fact, yet how often we forget to make use of it. Smith sent a double fault to me, and another double fault to Joad. He did not get in another ace service till halfway through the third set of a match which incidentally we won.

That night I thought hard and long. Could not this simple gambit of Joad's be extended to include other aspects of the game—to include all games? For me, it was the birth of gamesmanship.

II

THE PRE-GAME

" And now they smile at Paradine,
Who but would smile at Paradine?
(That man of games, called Paradine)
For the Gamesman came his way."

Paradine.

FOR THE EVOLUTION of gamesmanship I must refer the reader to my larger work on origins and history (see Appendix III).   But I do not propose to enlarge on the historical aspects here.

Let us start with a few simple exercises for beginners: and let us begin with the pre-game, for much of the most important gamesmanship play takes place before the game has started.   Yet if mistakes are made, there is plenty of time to recover.

The great second axiom of gamesmanship is now worded as follows: THE FIRST MUSCLE STIFFENED (in his opponent by the Gamesman) IS THE FIRST POINT GAINED.   Let us consider some of the processes of Defeat by Tension.

The standard method is known as the " flurry ".

The " flurry " is for use when changing in the locker-room before a rackets match, perhaps, or leaving home in your opponent's car for, say, a game of lawn tennis.   The object is to create a state of anxiety, to build up an atmosphere of muddled fluster.

Supposing, for instance, that your opponent has a small car. He kindly comes along to pick you up before the game. Your procedure should be as follows: (1) Be late in answering the bell. (2) Don't have your things ready. Appearing at last, (3) call *in an anxious or " rattled " voice* to wife (who need not, of course, be there at all) some taut last-minute questions about dinner. Walk down path and (4) realise you have forgotten shoes. Return with shoes; then just before getting into car pause (5) *a certain length of time* (see any threepenny edition of Bohn's *Tables*) and wonder (i) whether racket is at the club or (ii) whether you have left it " in the bath-room at top of the house ".

Like the first hint of paralysis, a scarcely observable fixing of your opponent's expression should now be visible. Now is the time to redouble the attack. Map-play can be brought to bear. On the journey let it be known that you " think you know a better way ", *which should turn out, when followed, to be incorrect and should if possible lead to a blind alley.* (See Fig. 2.)

Meanwhile, time is getting on. Opponent's tension should have increased. Psychological tendency, if not temporal necessity, will cause him to drive faster, and—behold! now the gamesman can widen his field and bring in carmanship by suggesting, with the minutest stiffening of the legs at corners, an unconscious tendency to put on the brakes, indicating an unexpressed desire to tell his opponent that he is driving not very well, and cornering rather too fast.

FIG. 2. Sketch plan to show specimen Wrong Route from
Maida Vale to Dulwich Covered Courts.

Note I.—The " flurry " is best used before still-ball games, especially golf, croquet or snooker. Anxious car-driving may actually improve opponent's execution in fast games, such as rackets or ping-pong.

Note II.—Beginners must not rush things. The smooth working of a " flurry " sequence depends on practice. The motions of pausing on the doorstep (" Have I got my gym shoes? "), hesitating on the running-board, etc., are exercises which I give my own students; but I always recommend that they practise the motions for at least six weeks, *positions only*, before trying it out with the car, suitcase and shoes.

Clothesmanship.

The " flurry " is a simple example. Simpler still, but leading to the most important subdivision of our subject, is the question of clothesmanship, or the " Togman ", as he used to be called.

The keen observer of the tennis-court incident described above would have noticed a marked disparity in clothes. The trousers of the young undergraduate players were well creased and clean, with flannel of correct colour, etc., etc. C. Joad, on the other hand, wore a shirt of deep yellow, an orange scarf to hold up his crumpled trousers, and—standing out very strongly, as I remember, in the hot June sunlight—socks of deep black.

Instinctively, Joad had demonstrated in action

what was to become the famous " Second Rule " of gamesmanship, now formulated as follows:

IF THE OPPONENT WEARS, OR ATTEMPTS TO WEAR, CLOTHES CORRECT AND SUITABLE FOR THE GAME, BY AS MUCH AS HIS CLOTHES SUCCEED IN THIS FUNCTION, BY SO MUCH SHOULD THE GAMESMAN'S CLOTHES FAIL.

Corollary: Conversely, if the opponent wears the wrong clothes, the gamesman should wear the right.

" If you can't volley, wear velvet socks," we Old Gamesmen used to say. The good-looking young athlete, perfectly dressed, is made to feel a fool if his bad shot is returned by a man who looks as if he has never been on a tennis-court before. His good clothes become a handicap by virtue of their very suitability.

It is true that against the new golf-club member, inclined to be modest and nervous, a professional turn-out can be effective. A well-worn but well-cut golf jacket and a good pair of mackintosh trousers can, in this situation, be of real value. (My own tip here is to take an ordinary left-hand glove, cut the thumb off, make a diamond-shaped hole on the back, and say, " Henry Cotton made this for me—he never plays with any other.")

Counter-Gamesmanship.

But the average gamesman must beware, at this point, of counter-gamesmanship. He may find himself up against an experienced hand, such as J. K. C.

FIG. 3. Clothesmanship: wrong clothes in which Miss E. Watson beat Mrs. de Greim in the Finals of the Waterloo Cup Croquet Tourney, 18th August 1902.

Dalziel, who, when going out to golf, used to keep two changes in the dickey of his car—one correct and the other incorrect. One golf-bag covered in zipps and with five woods, twelve irons and a left-handed cleek; a second bag containing only three irons and one wood, each with an appearance of string-ends tied round their necks. I always remember Jimmy Dalziel's " bent pin " outfit, as he used to call it. (" The little boy with the bent pin always catches more than the professional angler.") Many is the time I have scoured London with him to find a pair of odd shoe-laces. His plan was simple. If he found, at the club-house, that his opponent was rather humbly dressed, he would wear the smart outfit. If the conditions were reversed, out would come the frayed pin-stripe trousers, the stringy clubs and the fair-isle sweater.

" And I don't want a caddie," he would say.

Of course, in his correct clothes, he would automatically order a caddie, calling for " Bob ", and mumbling something about " Must have Bob. He knows my game. Caddied for me in the Northern Amateur."

III
THE GAME ITSELF

" East wind dhu blĕow
En-tout-cas dhu gëow."

Essex Saying.

SOME BASIC PLAYS

"How to win Games Without Being Able to Play Them." Reduced to the simplest terms, that is the formula, and the student must not at first try flights too far away from this basic thought.

To begin with, let him, say, carry on the " flurry " motive. Let him aim at tension. Let him, for instance, invent some " train which he would rather like to catch if the game was over by then ", but " doesn't want to hurry ".

Sportsmanship Play.

Remember the slogan: "THE GOOD GAMESMAN IS THE GOOD SPORTSMAN." The use of sportsmanship is, of course, most important. In general, with the athletic but stupid player, ex-rowing or ex-boxing, perhaps, who is going to take it out of you, by God, if he suspects you of being unsporting, extreme sportingness is the thing, and the instant waiving of any rule which works in your favour is the procedure.

On the other hand, playing against the introvert

27

crusty cynical type, remember that sportingness will be wasted on him. There must be no unsportingness on your part, of course; but a keen knowledge of little-known rules and penalties will cause him to feel he is being beaten at his own game. (See under " Croquet, rulesmanship in ".)

When questioned about the etiquette of gamesmanship—so important for the young player—I talk about Fidgets. If your adversary is nervy, and put off by the mannerisms of his opponent, it is unsporting, and therefore not gamesmanship, to go in, e.g., for a loud noseblow, say, at billiards, or to chalk your cue squeakingly, when he is either making or considering a shot.

On the other hand, a basic play, in perfect order, can be achieved by, say, whistling fidgetingly *while playing yourself*. And I once converted two down into two up when playing golf against P. Beard, known also as the leader of an orchestra, by constantly whistling a phrase from the Dorabella Variation with one note—always the same note—wrong.[1]

---

[1] It may be worth recalling that Elgar himself, when playing croquet against fellow-musicians, made use of the Horn *motiv* from the *Ring* :—

He would whistle this correctly except for the second note, substituting for A some inappropriate variant, often a slightly flattened D sharp, *sliding* up to it, from the opening note of the phrase :—

A voice from the past indeed. Yet have any of our modern experts in the music ploy really improved on this phrase, devised before Gamesmanship was formulated or even described?

A good general attack can be made by talking to your opponent about his own job, in the character of the kind of man who always tries to know more about your own profession than you know yourself.

Playing-for-Fun Play.

The good gamesman, like the good sportsman, never plays for large sums of money. But something can usually be made out of the situation if your opponent expresses a wish to play for the " usual half-crown ", or a wish not to do so. It is obviously easy for the gamesman to make his opponent feel awkward by countering his suggestion that they should play for stakes with a frank " Come, let's play for the fun of the game ". Alternatively, if your opponent refuses your offer to play for half a crown here is a neat counter:

LAYMAN: Half a crown on it? No, I'm not particularly anxious to play for money. What *is* the point? If one starts worrying about the pennies . . .

GAMESMAN: Exactly. If money is important to you, much better not.

LAYMAN: But I meant——

GAMESMAN: (*Friendly.*) Of course.

Nice Chapmanship.

A bigger subject which may be introduced here revolves round the huge question of nice chapmanship and its uses. (I refuse to use the hideous neologism " nicemanship " which I see much in evidence lately.)

Here is the general principle: that Being a Nice Chap *in certain circumstances* is valuable when playing against extremely young, public schooly players who are genuinely nice. A train of thought can be started in their minds to the effect that " it would be rather a rotten trick to beat old G. by too much ". Thereby that fatal " letting up " is inaugurated which can be the undoing of so many fine players. R. Lodge, at sixty-five, always said that he had never been beaten, in a key match, by any decently brought up boy under twenty-five, and that he could always " feel 'em out by their phizzes ".

Audience Play.

Nice chapmanship is, of course, closely associated with sportsmanship, especially in its relation to the question of playing or not playing to the audience. There is obviously some value in a good hearty " Have it again " early in the game (of darts, for instance), or the lawn tennis ball slammed into the net after the doubtful decision, especially if this is done so that your opponent can see through the ploy [1] but the onlookers cannot.

But the experienced gamesman knows that if he is playing to a small audience he must make up his mind whether he is going to play *to* the audience, or

[1] Sub-plays, or individual manoeuvres of a gambit, are usually referred to as " ploys". It is not known why this is.

whether he is going to retire behind an impersonal mask of modesty.

In general, the rule holds—LET YOUR ATTITUDE BE THE ANTITHESIS OF YOUR OPPONENT'S; and let your manner of emphasising this different attitude put him in the wrong.

For example, if your opponent is a great showman, assume (e.g., at snooker) an air of modest anonymity; be appreciative, even, of his antics; then quietly play your shot, so that the audience begins to say, " I prefer G.'s game. He gets on with it, any-how."

Per contra, when in play against a dour opponent, who studiously avoids all reaction to the audience, implying that " this is a match "—*then*, by all means be the " chap who doesn't care a damn " . . . though " Of course—sh!—old L. is taking this devilish seriously so I must keep a straight face ".

(There is some danger of counter-gamesmanship here. The layman, if he is wise, will pursue his poker-faced policy and you may find your assumption of ill-suppressed gaiety wearing thin. I have myself experienced a partial paralysis in this situation.)

So much for some of the principal general ploys. Now for some common technical phrases.

Ruggership and Ruggership Counter-play.

Under the heading of " Ruggership " comes all that great interplay of suggestion summarised in the phrase " Of course, this isn't my game ", with the implication that " this game is rather an amusing game, but not grand, dangerous and classical like my game . . .". If " my game " is rugger or polo or tennis (see under " Tennis players, how to press home advantage of, over lawn tennis players "), then very good work can be done with this gambit.

But it has severe weaknesses, and a promising gamesman in his second year may be able to counter with some such simple enquiry as this:

COUNTER-GAMESMAN (*with interest*): When did you *last play* rugger?

GAMESMAN: Oh! How long since actually play-ing? I wonder. . . . I was talking to Leggers the other day——

COUNTER-GAMESMAN: Yes, but how long is it since you played yourself? I mean what date, roughly, was it when you last held a ball in your hand?

GAMESMAN (*hard-pressed*): 1913.

COUNTER-GAMESMAN: A bit of a time. But that, I imagine, is one of the grand things about rugger. If you've ever kicked a rugger ball, at a prep school or home club, you feel that you're a rugger player for the rest of your life.

Much exaggerated praise has been churned out in honour of gamesmanship and its part in the building of the British character. Still, if we study the re-cords, they do reveal not a little of courage in the overcoming of apparently hopeless odds. I am thinking, of course, of G. Tearle—not the actor, but the croquet-player. And, indeed, some of the prettiest effects of gamesmanship are to be seen when an expert in, say, croquet, plays golf, it may be, off the same handicap, against a real expert in, say, rugger—a man who really has played rugger, twice capped for England. The rugger man certainly starts with a tremendous advantage. His name is a legend, his game is glorious. Croquet is considered, by the lay world, to be piddling. The two meet on the common ground of golf; and even golf, to the rugger man, is considered fairly piddling. Yet I have seen Tearle not only break down this view *but reverse it*, so that in the end the Rugger international would sometimes even be heard claiming that he came from croquet people, but that his character " was not suited to the game ".

Tearle by long practice actually made capital out of croquet. And let me add that Tearle's triumph demonstrates once again that it is in these long-drawn-out reversal tactics that training and the proper diet stand you in such good stead.

Counterpoint.

This phrase, now used exclusively in music, originally stood for Number Three of the general Principles of Gamesmanship. " PLAY AGAINST YOUR OPPONENT'S TEMPO." This is one of the oldest of gambits and is now almost entirely used in the form " My Slow to your Fast." E.g., at billiards, or snooker, or golf especially, against a player who makes a great deal of " wanting to get on with the game ", the technique is (1) to agree (Jeffreys always adds here " as long as we don't hurry on the shot "); (2) to hold things up by fifteen to twenty disguised pauses. Peg-top tees for golf were introduced by Samuel in '33 for this use. The technique is to tee the ball, frame up for the shot, and then at the last moment stop, pretend to push the peg a little further in or pull it a little further out, and then start all over again. At the next hole vary this with Samuel's " Golden Perfecto " peg tee, made in such a way that the ball,

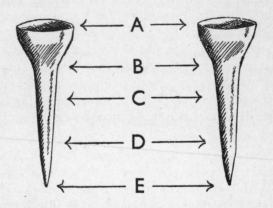

FIG. 4. Samuel's " Championship " (2d.) and " Golden Perfecto " (4/6) golf tees. A = " Cup ", B = " Neck ", C = " Upper Shaft ", D = " Lower Shaft ", E = Point or " Plungebill ".

after sitting still in the cup for two to three seconds, rolls off. (Fig. 4.)

Through the green, the usual procedure is to frame up for the shot and then decide on another club at the last moment.

> NOTE.—*Do not attempt to irritate partner by spending too long looking for your lost ball.* This is unsporting. But good gamesmanship which is also very good sportsmanship can be practised if the gamesman makes a great and irritatingly prolonged parade of spending extra time looking for his *opponent's* ball.

At billiards, the custom of arranging to be summoned to the telephone on fake calls, so as to break your opponent's concentration, is out of date now and interesting only as a reminder of the days when " couriers " were paid to gallop up to the old billiard halls for the same purpose. In snooker, the usual practice is to walk quickly up to the table, squat half down on the haunches to look at sight-lines, move to the other end of the table to look at sight-lines of balls which may come in to play later on in the break which you are supposed to be planning. Decide on the shot. Frame up for it, and then at the last moment see some obvious red shot which you had " missed ", and which your opponent and everybody else will have noticed before you moved to the table, and which they know is the shot you are going to play in the end anyhow.

For chess tempos see " Chess, tempi ".

" My To-morrow's Match ".

In a Key Friendly, or any individual match which you are particularly anxious to win, the best general approach (Rule IV) is the expression of *anxiety to play to-day, because of the match to-morrow.* Construct a story that you are playing A. J. du C. Masterman.[1] Or perhaps the name should be A. C. Swinburne (your opponent will feel he has vaguely heard of this name). Go on to say (if the game is golf)—" Do you mind if I practise using my Number One iron to-day? "—(no need to use it or even have one)—" as I want to know whether to take it to-morrow ". Take one practice shot after having picked up your ball, at a lost hole. Seek the advice of opponent. Ask him " What *he* would do if he found himself playing against a *really* long driver, like A. C. Swinburne ".

Game Leg (also known as " Crocked Ankle Play ", or " Gamesman's Leg " [2]).

" Limpmanship ", as it used to be called, or the exact use of minor injury, not only for the purpose of getting out of, but for actually winning difficult contests, is certainly as old as the mediaeval tourneys, the knightly combats, of ancient chivalry. Yet, nowadays, no device is more clumsily used, no gambit more often muffed. " I hope I shall be able to

---

[1] " Names impress according to the square of their initials."
[2] Usually shortened now into " Game Leg ".

give you a game," says the middle-aged golfer to his young opponent, turning his head from side to side and hunching up his shoulders. " My back was a bit seized up yesterday . . . this wind." How wretchedly weak. " O.K. My youth *versus* your age," says the young counter-gamesman to himself, and rubs this thought in with a variety of subsequent slanting references: " You ought to take it easy for a week or two ", etc. No, if use the hackneyed ankle gambit you must, let the injury be the result of a campaign in one of the wars, or a quixotic attempt to stop a runaway horse, at least.

But, here as so often, it is the *reply*, the counter, wherein the ploy of the gamesman can be used to best effect. Indeed, there is nothing prettier than the right use of an opponent's injury. There is the refusal to be put off even if the injury is genuine. There is the adoption of a game which, though apparently ignoring and indeed even favouring your opponent's disability, will yet benefit you in the end. In their own different ways, the " Two F's ", Frier and Frith-Morteroy, were the greatest masters of the art of " Countering the Crock ". No one who heard them will ever forget their apologies for sending a short one to the man with the twisted ankle, their excuses for the accidental lob in the sun against an opponent with sensitive eyes. But the Frith-Morteroy counter, though not for beginners, has more of grace, and needs more of explanation. Let it be lawn tennis—Frith's game. Frith against " Novice Gamesman ", we will call him.

Novice Gamesman is limping slightly. "Hopes
he can give F.-M. a game, but his rugger knee has
just been prodded back into place by old Coutts of
Welbeck Street". Right. F.-M. is full of sym-
pathy. F.-M. sends not a single short one. In fact
he does nothing whatever. His supporters become
anxious—and then—during, say, the *first* game of the
second set, while they are changing sides Frith is
heard to say (on arriving at point K—see Fig. 5)
"Ooo!" sharply.

NOVICE GAMESMAN: What's that?
FRITH-MORTEROY: Nothing.   Nothing.   I
        thought——
N. G. (*further away*): What did you say?
F.-M.: Nothing.

The games continues. But at that next cross over,
Frith says "Ow!" (point S, Fig. 5). He pauses a
minute, and stands as if lost in thought.

N. G.: What's up?
F.-M.: Nothing. Half a moment.
N. G.: Something wrong?
F.-M. (*rubs his chest with his knuckles*): No. No.
        It's only the old pump.
N. G.: Pump?
F.-M.: Yes. The ancient ticker.
N. G.: What—heart?
F.-M.: I'm supposed not to be using it full out
        at the moment. Only a temporary thing.
N. G.: Good Lord.

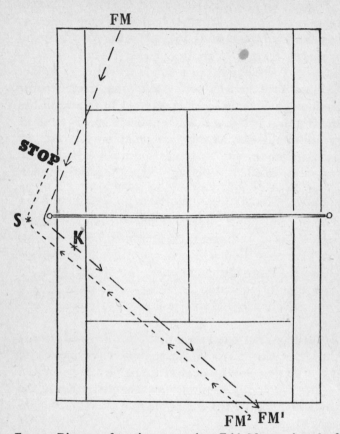

FIG. 5. Diagram of tennis court to show Frith-Morteroy's path of changing, and the position S from which he makes his " echo " attack, in Morteroy Counter Game Leg play. Point K on the line FM–FM¹ is the position from which the demi-cry is made (see text). At point S, on the line FM², the full cry is made (see text). " STOP " marks the usual position for the actual verbal interchange or " parlette ".

F.-M.: It's all right now!

N. G.: Good.

F.-M.: Couple of crocks!

N. G.: Well. Shall we get on?

" *Couple* of crocks." Observe the triple thrust against the Novice Gamesman. (1) Frith establishes the fact that he, also, labours under a handicap; (2) the atmosphere which Novice Gamesman has built up with so much restraint, but so much labour—the suggestion of silent suffering—is the precise climate in which Frith is now going to prosper, and (3)—most important of all—Frith has won the gamesmanship part of the contest already, set and match, by sportingly waiting, say twenty-five minutes, before revealing his own somewhat worse disability. Novice Gamesman having mentioned his rugger knee—a stale type of infliction anyhow—is made to look a fool and a fusser. More, he is made to look unsporting.

I believe it is true to say that once Frith-Morteroy had achieved this position, he was never known to lose a game. He made a special study of it—and I believe much of his spare time was spent reading the medical books on the subject of minor cardiac weaknesses.

Jack Rivers Opening.

After this most successful of basic plays, may I dare to end this chapter with a very simple but favourite gambit of my own?

I call it the Jack Rivers Opening. I have written elsewhere of the sporting–unsporting approach, always to be revered as the parent of modern gamesman play. But if sporting–unsporting is vaguely regarded as a thing of the past, the gamesman knows that it is a habit of thought still rooted in many British players.

Perhaps the most difficult type for the gamesman to beat is the man who indulges in pure play. He gets down to it, he gets on with it, he plays each shot according to its merits, and his own powers, without a trace of exhibitionism, and no by-play whatever. In golf, croquet or ping-pong—golf especially—he is liable to wear you down by playing the " old aunty " type of game.

My only counter to this, which some have praised, is to invent, early in the game or before it has started, an imaginary character called " Jack Rivers ". I speak of his charm, his good looks, his fine war record and his talent for games—and, " by the way, he is a first-class pianist as well ". Then, a little later: " I like Jack Rivers's game ", I say. " He doesn't care a damn whether he wins or loses so long as he has a good match."

Some such rubbish as this, although at first it may not be effective, often wears down the most successfully cautious opponent, *if the method is given time to soak in.* Allow your opponent to achieve a small lead, perhaps, by his stone-walling methods; and the chances are that—even if he has only been hearing about Jack Rivers for thirty minutes—he will begin to think: " Well, perhaps I am being a bit of a stick-in-the-mud." He feels an irrational desire to play up to what appears to be your ideal of a good fellow. After all, he remembers, hadn't he been once chaffed for breaking a window with a cricket-ball when he was on holiday at Whitby? He himself was a bit mad once. Soon he is throwing away point after point by adopting a happy-go-lucky, hit-or-miss method which doesn't suit his game in the least.

Meanwhile *you* begin to play with pawky steadiness, and screen this fact by redoubling your references to Jack Rivers. You talk of the way in which Jack, too, loved to open his shoulders for a mighty smite, landing him in trouble as often as not; but the glorious thing about him was that he didn't care two hoots for that . . . and so long as he had a good smack, and a good game . . ., etc.

So much for the Principal Plays, in gamesmanship. Now for the other gambits which must be brought into play as the game progresses.

IV

WINMANSHIP

" . . . for the love of winning . . ."

> *Life and Laughter 'Mongst the People of*
> *North-Western Assam*, by P. V. Chit-
> terje; *trans*. Evadne Butterfield.

THIS is a short chapter. The assiduous student of
gamesmanship has little time for the *minutiae* of the
game itself—little opportunity for learning how to
play the shots, for instance. His skill in stroke-
making may indeed be almost non-existent. So that
the gamesman who finds himself winning in the early
stages of the match is sometimes at a loss. Therefore, although I am aware that this book must stand
or fall by its all-important Chapter VI on " Losemanship ", yet this seems to me the place to set down
a few words of help and friendly advice to the winning gamesman, to help him keep his lead; to assist
him to maintain his advantage, and rub his opponent's
face in the dirt.

A Note on Concentration.

Very often the opponent will show signs, just as he
is beginning to lose, of being irritated by distractions.
At golf, " somebody has moved ". At billiards,
" somebody talked ". Take this opportunity of

making him feel that he is not really a player at all by talking on these lines:

> " Somebody yelling, did you say? Do you know, I didn't notice it. I'm a fool at games. Don't seem to be able to be aware of anything outside them, when I'm playing the shot. I remember, once, Joyce Wethered was putting. 18th green—semi-final. An express train went by within fifteen feet of her nose.
>
> " ' How did you manage to sink that putt—with that train . . .?'
>
> " ' What train?' she said."

Always tell the same story to the same man, for your example. (See under " Story, constant repetition of, to the same person.")

When to Give Advice.

In my own view (but compare Motherwell) there is only one correct time when the gamesman can give advice: and that is when the gamesman has achieved a *useful* though not necessarily a *winning* lead. Say three up and nine to play at golf, or, in billiards, sixty-five to his opponent's thirty. Most of the accepted methods are effective. E.g., in billiards, the old phrase serves. It runs like this:

GAMESMAN: Look . . . may I say something?
LAYMAN: What?
GAMESMAN: *Take it easy.*
LAYMAN: What do you mean?
GAMESMAN: I mean—you know how to make the

44

strokes, but you're stretching yourself on the rack all the time. Look. Walk up to the ball. Look at the line. And make your stroke. Comfortable. Easy. It's as simple as that.

In other words, the advice *must be vague*, to make certain it is not helpful. But, in general, if properly managed, the mere giving of advice is sufficient to place the gamesman in a practically invincible position.

NOTE.—According to some authorities the advice should be quite genuine and perfectly practical.

When to be Lucky.

The uses of the last of the three basic plays for winmanship are, I think, no less obvious, though I believe this gambit is less used than the other, no doubt because a certain real skill in play is involved, making it a little out of place in the gamesman world. I have worded the rule as follows. LET THE GAMESMAN'S ADVANTAGE OVER AN OPPONENT APPEAR TO BE THE RESULT OF LUCK, NEVER OF PLAY. Always sporting, the good gamesman will say:

" I'm afraid I was a bit lucky there . . . the balls are running my way. It's extraordinary, isn't it, how once they start running one way, they go on running one way, all through an entire game. I know it's impossible according to the law of averages . . ."

and so on, till your opponent is forced to break in with a reply. Unless he sees through the gambit and counter-games, he is likely to feel an ebbing of confidence if he can be made to believe that it is not your play (which he knows is liable to collapse) but Fate, which is against him.

Yet in spite of the ease with which most games-players can be persuaded that they are unlucky, I know the difficulties of this gambit: and as I have had many complaining letters from all parts of the country from gamesmen saying: "They can't do it", "What's the point?", "No good", etc., I will end this chapter with a few notes:

NOTE I.—The best shot to practise with cue and ivories is undoubtedly the Imitation Fluke. E.g., in billiards, play for an in-off the red top left of a kind which will give colour to your apology that you meant to pot the red top right. A. Boult (the snooker player, not the conductor) demonstrates a shot, suitable for volunteer only, in which he pots the black while apparently framing up to hit a ball of inferior scoring value (e.g., the blue). (See Fig. 6.)

A good tip, says Boult, is to chalk the end of the cue ostentatiously, while apologising after making the shot.

NOTE II.—In my pamphlet for the British Council I listed eighteen ways of saying "Bad luck". I do not believe there are more.

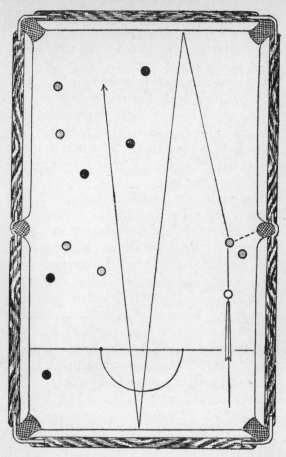

FIG. 6. Diagram of billiards table to show Disguised Fluke play. Key: Black balls = red balls; shaded balls = coloured balls; white ball = white ball; end of cue = end of cue. Player has framed up as if to hit blue (on extreme right) but actually pots black (ball on extreme right but one). Straight line = path of white ball after impact (leaving an easy red). Dotted line = path of black into middle pocket.

Note III (For advanced students only).—
Different from fluke play, though sometimes
confused with it, is the demonstration of another
kind of advantage over an opponent in which
the gamesman tries to prove that he is favoured
not by good luck but by *a fortunate choice of
instruments*. To get away from text-book for-
mulae, let me explain this by example.

In golf, for instance. You find yourself two
up at the fifth hole. You wish to make certain
of your advantage.

Supposing, for whatever reason, you hit your
drive; and supposing you hit it five or prefer-
ably ten yards farther than your opponent.
Procedure: walk off the tee *with* opponent, in
the normal method of the two-up walk-off,
conversing, and listening rather charmingly to
what he says, etc. (See Number Twelve in my
Twenty-five Methods of Tee-leaving: Scribners,
August 1935.) As you approach the balls on
the fairway, but before parting company (see
Fig. 7) say, " Much of a muchness ". Opponent will then say over his shoulder:

" You're ten yards farther at least."

" So I am," you say.

Nearing the green you start thinking aloud in
his presence.

" Funny. I thought those drives were level.
It's that ball of mine."

" What are you using? Ordinary two-dot,
isn't it? "

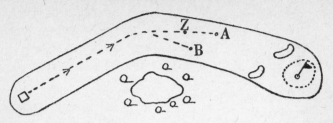

FIG. 7. Diagram of golf hole. A = point reached by Gamesman's drive. B = opponent's drive. Z = point on arrival at which Gamesman commences Gamesplay or "Parlette".

"Oh, no—no—that's how it's been repainted. Underneath it's a Madfly."

"Madfly?"

"Madfly. Pre-war only. It goes like sin. Really does put ten yards on to your shot. I'll see if I can get you one. Honestly, I hardly feel it's fair of me to play with it."

With proper management the gamesman can wreak far more havoc by suggesting that he has the advantage of a better ball, than by demonstrating that he has a better swing.

Tennis rackets strung with a special gut giving out a particularly high "ping", suggesting a tigerish resilience, are made by dealers who cater for this sort of thing. G. Odoreida, on his first appearance at St. Ives, brought with him a racket in which a stretch of piano wire, tuned to high G, was substituted for one of the ordinary strings. When "testing his racket" before play, he plucked the piano wire, adding smilingly: "I like something you can hit with."

49

A propos of this, an amusing correspondence followed with " Wagger "—W.A.G.A., the West Australian Gamesmen's Association—which august body considered this action ungamesmanlike.

V

LUNCHEONSHIP

"For gamesmen work i' th' playtime,
To pledge their souls away."
Plainsong of Perkins, Gent.

THE WAY of the gamesman is hard, his training
strict, his progress slow, his disappointments many.
If he is to succeed, he must, for instance, read our
next chapter, on " Losemanship ", with something
more than concentration. He must *believe* that the
precepts it contains are effective, and *trust* that they
make sense, and *want* to put them into action.

So let us, as they say, " take a breather ". Let us
turn for a moment to what I always consider to be
the lighter side of the subject, even if in all earnest
many a match is won by a knowledge of what to say
during the meal interval, and how to say it.

In golf, in the all-day lawn tennis or badminton
tournament, in cricket or bowls, the luncheon interval is the ideal time in which to make up lost ground.

Drinkmanship.

This huge subject, the notes for which I have been
collecting for so many years that they threaten
already to overstep the bounds of a single volume,
can scarcely even be defined within the limits of a

51

chapter. Put in the simplest possible words, the art
of drinkmanship is the art of imparting uneasiness
to your opponent by making a show of (1) readiness
or (2) reluctance to " go shares " in the hire of a
court, payment for taxi, payment for meal, but above
all in the matter of " standing your round " of alco-
holic drink; the art, moreover, of inseminating in the
mind of your opponent, by this action, that he has
paid more than his share, or, more rarely, less than
his share; the whole gambit to be played with the
object of setting up (by this action) a train of uneasiness in the mind, with subsequent bewilderment
at the commencement or resumption of the game.

The rarer form (" Counter-drink Play ") is for use
only in the following situation, where, however, it is a
gambit of the first value.

Take a young opponent (optimum age: twenty-
two). He must be pleasant, shy and genuinely
sporting. (The Fischer Test will tell you whether
his apparent character is real or assumed—see
" Nice Chapmanship ", p. 29). Then (1) Place
him by the bar and stand him a drink. (2) When he
suggests " the other half ", refuse in some such words
as these, which should be preceded by a genuinely
kindly laugh: " Another one? No thanks, old
laddie. . . . *No*, I certainly won't let you buy me
one. No—I don't want it." Then (3) a minute or
two later, when his attention is distracted, buy him,
and yourself, the second drink. The boy will feel
bound to accept it, yet this enforced acceptance
should cause him some confusion, and a growing

thought, if the gambit has been properly managed and the after-play judicious, that he has been fractionally put in his place and decimally treated as if he was a juvenile, and more than partially forced into the position of being the object of generosity.

Straight drinkmanship, *of a kind*, is known all over the world and, of course, long before Simpson and I incorporated it in gamesplay, the fellow who " was shy of his round " was the menace of club and pub. But genuine drinkmanship is very different, if only because no true gamesman is, I hope, ever either mean or bad mannered.

In my larger work I have planned twelve chapters for the twelve principal drink plays—and while I was working out the details of dialogue and positional play I often asked myself: " What is *the true purpose* of the tactic—what is it all about? "

Whatever the details, remember the basic drill. (1) Remember always that (except in the case of the Nice Young Chap) " ONE DRINK UP IS ONE HOLE (OR IN LAWN TENNIS ONE GAME) UP". But (2) Remember also that to achieve the best results your opponent should not realise that you have avoided paying for a drink *at once*. Optimum realisation time: standing on the first tee, or, better still, when he makes his first bad shot. Therefore the ordinary escape tactics, e.g., (i) turning aside to ask " was that telephone call for me? "; (ii) going vague; (iii) producing a treasury note too big to be changed, etc.—these are not successful against an opposing drinkman of average recovering power.

NOTE.—After your opponent has lost the game, angered by the thought that he has been out-witted in the bar-room—*then*, after the game, make him still more annoyed by saying: " By the way, I owe you a drink—and a large one." You will thereby not only prepare the ground for the next match by obscurely irritating your man with *Winner's Heartiness*: you will at the same time maintain the gamesman's standard of hospitality and good manners.

Guestmanship.

Elwyn Courthope—brother of G. L.—made a special study of " putting your man in the drink-drums ", as we used to say at Prince's (the tie of which I still wear, though I was never a member [1]). But his one-sidedness enforced this penalty on his game: that it was only successful against opponents at his own club or in hotel or pub. As a guest, where drinks were going to be bought for him any-how, he was lost.

That is, of course, why G. L. Courthope—known from time immemorial as " Court "—invented guestmanship, of which, in spite of the later experi-ments of Thomas and Riezenkühl, he can justly be called the Father.

The object of guestmanship is difficult to achieve.

[1] At Oxford, though never a blue, I used to wear a blue's tie—particularly when playing games against nicemen who knew I had no right to wear the honour. This simple trick, which is said by psychologists to induce the "pseudo-schizophrenic syndrome", or doubt, was most effective in moving-ball games.

The host is at an advantage. He is playing on his home ground. He knows the ropes. He has armies of friends. There are plenty of opportunities for making his guest feel out of it. But by the time Court had finished with him, an average host would wonder whether he was a host in any valid sense except the unpleasant one of having to pay: indeed, he would begin to wonder whether he was really a member of his own club.

G. L. used to start, very quietly, (A) by some such question as this: (1) " Have you got a card-room here? " (knowing that, as a matter of fact, they hadn't). Or (2) (In the Wash-place): " Do you find you manage all right with two showers, in the summer? " He would then (B) find some member whom he knew, but his host didn't, and carry on an animated conversation with this man. Discover " at the last moment " that his host had never met him. Introduce them, with surprised apologies, and tell the host later that he really must get to know this fellow—his interest and influence, etc. At luncheon, Court would always know some special ale, or even only a special mustard, the existence of which in the club, after fifteen years use of it, the host had rather lamely to explain he knew nothing about. Court then would ask why X was on the Committee, and why Y wasn't, and make use of a host of facts which he had been able to pick up from a lightning study of lists, menus, pictures of former captains, etc., which he had studied during his host's temporary absence paying some bill.

VI

LOSEMANSHIP

" . . . For the glory of the gamesman who's a loseman
in the game."

THE READER WHO has thoroughly absorbed the first
four chapters will know something of the funda-
mentals. He will be prepared, I believe, now, to
take that little extra step which will put him on the
way to being a gamesman. And he will realise that
he cannot comprehend *the thing itself*, unless he knows
how to turn the tide of defeat, and, with alertness and
courage, with humour and goodwill, learn to play for
the fun and glory of the gamesplay.

Straight now to the underlying principle of winning the losing game. What is the chief danger from
the opponent who is getting the better of you? Over
and above the advantage in score comes the fact that
he is in the *winning vein*. He is playing at his best.
Yet this is but one end of a balance. It is your job
to turn the winning vein into a *losing streak*.

The Primary Hamper.

There is only one rule : BREAK THE FLOW. This act
—for it must be thought of as a positive *action*, dynamic
not static—may bear directly on the game itself

(*Primary Hamper*) or the net may be cast wider, in a direction apparently far removed from the main target, in an attempt to entangle the character, or even to bring forces to bear from your knowledge of the private life and intimate circumstances of your opponent's everyday existence (*Secondary Hamper*).

To take the simplest example of a Primary, let us begin with an illustration from golf (the " gamesgame of gamesgames ").

This is the rule.

Rule I: [1] CONSCIOUS FLOW IS BROKEN FLOW. To break the flow of the golfer who is three up at the turn, select a moment during the playing of the tenth in the following way. This moment must be prepared for by not less than three suggestions that he is " playing well ", " hitting the ball grandly ", etc., made at, say, the second, fifth and ninth holes. Then as opponent walks up to play his shot from fairway, speak as follows:

GAMESMAN: I believe I know what it is.

LAYMAN: What do you mean?

GAMESMAN: I believe I know what you're doing.

LAYMAN: What?

GAMESMAN: Yes. Why you're hitting them. Straight left arm at the moment of impact.

LAYMAN (*pleased*): I know what you mean. Oh, God, yes! If the left arm isn't coming down straight like a flail——

GAMESMAN: Rather.

---

[1] In all previous editions Rule I was Rule II.

LAYMAN: Like a whip——

GAMESMAN: It's centrifugal force.

LAYMAN: Well, I don't know. Yes, I suppose it is. But if there's the least suggestion of— of——

GAMESMAN: A crooked elbow—(*L. is framing up to play his shot*). Half a sec. Do you mind if I come round to this side of you? I want to see you play that shot . . . (*L. hits it*) . . . Beauty. (*Pause*).

LAYMAN: Good Lord, yes! You've got to have a straight left arm.

GAMESMAN: Yes. And even that one wasn't as clean as some of the shots you've been hitting. . . .

LAYMAN (*pleased*): Wasn't it? (*Doubtful*). Wasn't it? (*He begins to think about it*).

There is nothing rigid about the last few lines of this dialogue, which are capable of some modification. But the shape—Praise-Dissection-Discussion-Doubt—is the same for all shots and for all games. I often think the possibilities of this gambit alone prove the superiority of games to sports, such as, for instance, rowing, where self-conscious analysis of the stroke can be of actual benefit to the stroke maker.

Potter's Improvement on the Primitive Hamper.

The superiority of Primary Hamper over Primitive Hamper needs no elaboration. But it is worth remembering that some of the earliest tentative ploys in what Toynbee calls, in an amusing essay, the Palæogamesman period, were directed to this essential *breaking of the flow*. They consisted of such naïve devices as tying up a shoe-lace in a prolonged manner, after the opponent at squash or lawn tennis had served two or three aces running; the extended noseblow, with subsequent mopping up not only of the nose and surrounding surfaces, but of imaginary sweat from the forehead and neck as well; leaving your driver on the tee and going back for it, etc., etc.

My own name has been associated—against my will [1]—with an attempt to bring the Primitive Hamper up to date. The essence of the modern approach is the making of the pause *as if for the sake of your opponent's game*. E.g., at lawn tennis, opponent having won six consecutive points.:

GAMESMAN (*calling*): Wait a minute.

OPPONENT: What's wrong?

GAMESMAN (*turning to look at a child walking slowly along a path a hundred yards behind the court. Then turning back*): Those damn kids.

OPPONENT: Where?

GAMESMAN: Walking across your line of sight.

OPPONENT: What?

GAMESMAN: I said "Walking across your line of sight".

OPPONENT: I can't see anyone.

---

[1] I wished it to be called "Linlithgow", after that great Viceroy and good man.

GAMESMAN: WHAT?

OPPONENT: I say I CAN'T SEE ANYONE.

GAMESMAN (*continues less distinctly*) . . . bang in the line of sight . . . ought to be shot . . ., etc.

Or, in a billiard room, your opponent has made a break of eight, and looks as if he may be going to make eight more. If two or more people are present they are likely not to be especially interested in the game, and quietly talking, perhaps. Or moving teacups. Or glasses. Simulate annoyance, *on your opponent's behalf*, with the onlookers. An occasional irritated glance will prepare the way; then stop your opponent and say:

GAMESMAN (*quietly*): Are they worrying you?

LAYMAN: Who?

GAMESMAN: Compton and Peters.

LAYMAN: It's all right.

Or say to the whisperers, half, but only half, jokingly:

Hi, I say. This is a billiard room, you know. Dead silence, please!

This should not only put an end to opponent's break. It may cause him, if young, to be genuinely embarrassed.

Further " Improved Primitives " are (*a*) the removal of an imaginary hair from opponent's ball, when he is in play; (*b*) licking of finger to pick up speck of dust, etc. For squash, badminton, rackets, tennis or indoor lawn-tennis courts or fives-courts in rainy weather, it will usually be possible to find a small patch on to which water is dripping. When opponent is *winning, particularly if he is winning his service*, become suddenly alarmed for his safety.

1. Make futile efforts to remove water with handkerchief or by kicking at it.
2. Talk of danger of slipping, and
3. If necessary call for sawdust, which, of course, will be unobtainable.

The Secondary Hamper.

(NOTE.—This section is for *advanced students only*. All others move straight to Chapter VII. Students who have made no progress at all should go back to the beginning.)

The Secondary Hamper is still in an early stage of development: and there are at least three London Clubs where it is not used. As followers of a recent *Daily Telegraph* correspondence will know, the Secondary Hamper is not allowed on the G.W.R.[1] But my view, for what it is worth, is that Bristol will have to follow where Manchester led.

The *object* of the secondary hamper is to bring to bear on the game *private life*—your own or your opponent's. The whole ploy is based, of course, on the proved fact that in certain circumstances, and at certain times, such a simple remark as " We're very

[1] Gamesmanship West Regional.

lucky in our new son-in-law " may have a profound effect on the game. Or take such an apparently innocent sequence as this:

GAMESMAN: I was fortunate enough to meet your daughter on Sunday.

LAYMAN: Yes, indeed—I know. She told me.

GAMESMAN: What wonderful hair—a real Titian.

LAYMAN: Oh—no—that can't have been my daughter—that was Ethel Baird.

GAMESMAN: *Really*. But I thought I was talking to your——

LAYMAN: You were, but that was earlier on.

GAMESMAN: *Was* it—but what was the colour of your daughter's hair?

LAYMAN: Well—a sort of brown——

GAMESMAN: Of course. Of course. Of course. Of course.

Simple and ordinary as such a conversation seems to be, the master gamesman, in play against the less experienced, can turn it to his advantage. A feather-weight distraction . . . a fleeting annoyance . . . a handicap of a sort if only because the victim is made to feel that he *is being got at* in some way.

These dialogue attacks or " parlettes " led to many other secondaries, still more intimately personal in approach, including especially, of course, those taught me by Edward Grice just before the recent World War.[1] I now use them more than any other gamesmanship gambit: and Grice himself was good

[1] In 1937.

enough to say, in 1939, that the basic " Second Secondary " which I evolved for my own use was not less useful than one or two of his own. Nothing was printed, and then the war came, and I remember telling my wife with some pride that there was a security stop on my little invention! So now, in 1947, it appears in print for the first time.

The idea grew out of a memory from my pre-gamesman days. My friend J. J. (as I will call him) and I played croquet together in a relentless and un-ending series of singles. In those days J. J. could beat me. But there was a certain memorable spring, a certain March to June, when the upper hand was just as regularly with me.

What had happened? I searched through old letters and diaries, to try to find the cause. The explanation was simple.

During those three months, J. J., for the first and last time in his life, had had a very marked success with a girl I was fond of. J. J., in fact, had, or felt that he had, snatched this girl away from me. I may have been upset. I believe that—in so far as one could be upset in the midst of a croquet series— I did feel it. But whatever the facts, J. J. *found himself constitutionally unable to win his games against me during this period*. With his blue and black both on the last hoop, he would unaccountably allow me to hoop and peg out one of his balls. Or he would fail to get started at all, till I was half way round with my red, his two clips remaining on the first hoop pathetically, forlornly and lopsidedly perched like a fox-terrier's ears.

And now, in a flash, I realised the cause of J. J.'s lapse. He could not bring himself to strike a man when he was down, *particularly since he himself was the cause of the trouble*, or so he believed.

From the games point of view, it was a fortunate situation for me. J. J. never quite regained his superiority—and, in fact, in our present series I am three up. Years later, in my gamesman days, it struck me that what was successful before, might be successful again. In the autumn of 1935 I again found myself engaged in a long series of singles against my old games friend " Dr. Bill ", as I will call him. This time the game was golf; but again I found myself in the position of regular loser.

I chose the day and the time. I had suffered my seventh consecutive defeat. The conversation ran something like this. I spoke of a mutual friend, to whom I had purposely introduced Dr. Bill six weeks before. Her name was Patricia Forrest.[1]

S. P. (*suddenly, à propos of nothing*): What a grand girl Pat is.

DR. BILL: Yes, isn't she? You see quite a bit of her, don't you?

S. P.: Well . . . we're kind of old friends.

DR. BILL: I thought so.

(*Pause*).

S. P.: Which exactly describes it. Alas!

---

[1] I have tried, in this book, to avoid pseudonyms. The reader will forgive me if on this occasion I break my rule.

DR. BILL: What do you mean?

S. P.: Well—you know.

DR. BILL: What do you mean, sort of—— ?

S. P. (*gruffly*): I shall always like her—very much.

DR. BILL: I'm sure I would if I knew her.

(Pause).

S. P. (*with glance*): She was talking about you the other day.

DR. BILL (*slight pause*): Me?

S. P. (*giving him warm-hearted, Major Dobbin look*): I think she likes you, bless you. (*At this point a hand may be laid on the forearm. But a transient grip of the elbow is better. See Fig.* 8.)

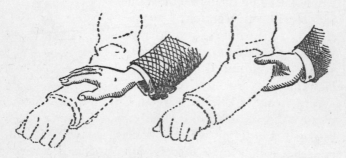

FIG. 8. Advanced Secondary Hamper (1). (*a*) Hand laid on forearm (right). (*b*) Transient grip of the elbow (better).

DR. BILL: I don't think she even knows I exist——

S. P.: On the contrary, she's very well aware of it indeed . . . damn your eyes!

"Damn your eyes!" is said, of course, in a friendly, nicechap voice. If opponent is still mystified, then

65

Fig. 9.

Advanced Secondary Hamper (2).

(*a*) Dandelion swing (wrong).
(*b*) Dandelion swing (right).

gamesman should (1) become de-
spondent and silent or (2) he
should knock off head of dandelion
with any iron club either by means
of (*a*) an ordinary rough golf
stroke, or (*b*) better, with a one-
armed " windmill " swing (see
Fig. 9).

(*a*) Wrong.

Now what happens? Your Dr. Bill will feel
pleased and flattered *as a ladies' man*. " I am a success with Pat " (or whoever she is), he will say to
himself. But being a success with Patricia is a very
long way from, in fact definitely opposed to, being
at great pains to defeat your unfortunate and
unsuccessful rival at anything so comparatively
trivial [1] as a game. Indeed, arranged properly the
gambit will lead him to feel that having pinched your

---

[1] I do not apologise for " comparatively trivial ". Love is more
important than games. And I also believe that love is more
important than gamesmanship.

(*b*) Right.

girl it is more or less incumbent on him to allow you to win.

NOTE.—There is of course an obvious counter-game to this gambit, and it is a fascinating " show " for the spectators to watch two games-men trying to prove that it is the other one whom the girl really prefers. Leonards and McDirk used to draw a big crowd when they were fighting out a match on these lines.

I was once dangerously counter-gamed in the

teeth of my own gambit. My opponent cut in on the words "We're very old friends" with a new line of thought which ran as follows:

COUNTER-GAMESMAN: Well, I ought to play well to-day.

GAMESMAN: You always do. But what's up? Anything special?

COUNTER-GAMESMAN: I'm a free man.

GAMESMAN: Splendid. What do you mean?

COUNTER-GAMESMAN: I'm one of the idle classes.

GAMESMAN (*genuinely interested*): What—you haven't left the North British and United?

COUNTER-GAMESMAN (*stiffly*): They are very sorry. They are cutting down staff.

GAMESMAN: You mean you've got the sack?

In the face of this disaster to my friend it was hopeless to go on with the "You're a lucky, fellow" sequence. And I'm bound to admit that my contra-counter ("Well, we must moan together: the doctor says this is the last game I shall ever be able to play") seemed lame and forced. But the small band of us who are interested in this branch of the game, believe me, will continue to improve and experiment; though bold man would he be who could boast a defence against every conceivable counter-hamper.

Hampettes.

"Hampettes", or minor hampers, exist in plenty. Many of them are of occasional use to the losing

gamesman. Many of them come under the heading
" Of course, this isn't really my game " (see
" Ruggership ", p. 31). While playing squash,
let it be known that rackets is *your Game*, and
that squash is that very different thing, a game
which you find it occasionally amusing to play
at, for the fun of the thing. R. Simpson first
drew my attention to this gambit when I was
playing lawn tennis with him on a damp grass
court on the borders of Lyme Regis. I happened
to be seeing the ball and for once in my life
really was driving it on to that precious square
foot in the back-hand corner of the base line. After
one of these shots, Simpson was " carried away "
enough to tap his racket twice on the ground and
cry " chase better than half a yard ". I only dimly
realised that this was an expression from tennis itself,
which had slipped out by accident; that he was
familiar with the great original archetype of lawn
tennis, compared with which lawn tennis itself (he
wished to make and succeeded in making me under-
stand) was a kind of French cricket on the sands at
Southend.

I lost that game But I learnt my lesson. I walked
about the real tennis-court at Blackfriars (Manchester) two or three times " in order to be taught the
game ". I took lessons from the pro (I showed no
aptitude). I put by a few shillings in order to buy
that most gamesmanly shaped, ungainlily twisted
racket. I keep it in the office. And although it has
never hit a ball since those Manchester days, I make

admirable use of that racket almost every week of my life.

The Natural Hampette.

There is a hampette which I like to use against a certain type of player. It has no official name: it obeys no code and no rule. Among my small group of students I used to call it " After All ".

" After all there are more important things than games." There are often occasions, when losing against a particularly grim, competent, unemotional and ungamesmanageable opponent, when this motion may be suggested, as a last resort.

I use it in golf. Without warning, I assume the character of a nature rambler. " Good lord," I say, bending down suddenly and examining the turf on the side of the bunker, into which, for once, my opponent has strayed. " Good lord. I didn't know Bristle Agrostis grew in Bucks."

LAYMAN: What's that?
GAMESMAN: Look. Lovely little grass, with a sharp leaf. It ought to be sandy here.
LAYMAN: Well, it's sandy in the bunker.
GAMESMAN: No, I mean it's supposed only to grow on sandy soil. Ah well!

Then later:

GAMESMAN: What a day! (*Breathing deeply*). And what a sky!
LAYMAN: It's going to rain if we don't look sharp.

GAMESMAN: That's right. It's a real Constable
    sky. That's the glorious thing about golf,
    it brings you closer to England.[1]

LAYMAN: How d'you mean?

GAMESMAN (*breathes deeply*).

Layman's game may not yet have been affected,
but a tiny seed of doubt has been planted. Is he
missing something? Also, his opponent is showing a
suspicious lack of anxiety over being two down. A
little later you pick up a loose piece of mud behind
your ball, as if to throw it out of the way, and then
you suddenly stop, and look at the scrap of muck.

GAMESMAN: Look. Pellet of the tawny owl.

LAYMAN: Pellet?

GAMESMAN: Yes. I wonder if she has rodings
    round here.

LAYMAN: Rodings?

GAMESMAN: Yes, there has been a great increase of
    the tawny owl in Wilts., and if we could
    show that she was something more than an
    irregular visitor in Kent it would be good.

LAYMAN: But this is Berkshire.

GAMESMAN (*thoughtfully*): Exactly.

LAYMAN: I suppose they're useful. (*Layman now
    feels he must take a halting part in the conversa-
    tion.*) I mean—mice——

GAMESMAN: As a matter of fact we *don't know*.
    The chances at present are fifty-fifty.

[1] This phase of the play is sometimes called Sussexmar.ship. In
a book such as this, which deals with First Principles, it has been
my aim to use as few technical terms as possible.

LAYMAN: Oh, yes. Chances of what?
GAMESMAN: We're working on her now. All
    amateur work. The amateurs have done
    wonderful work. Absolutely splendid.

This conversation, with identical wording, will do
of course for any bird. If a faint crack is now
apparent in your opponent's game, redouble your
references to the " marvellous work of the amateurs "
whenever you are in earshot. That this gambit (the
" *natural hampette* ", I want it to be called) works, is a
matter of fact. Why it works, is one of the mysteries
of gamesmanship.

> NOTE I.—This technique has no connection
> with the ploy of the gamesman who says
> "Whoosh! I wish I'd got my ·22 with me ",
> whenever he sees a bird get up.
>
> See in this same series *Bird Gamesmanship*,
> especially the chapter on Game Birdmanship.
> Also the pamphlet published by the Six Squires
> Press—*Big Gamesmanship and Blood Sportsmanship:
> Fact and Fancy*. 8*d*., and the graph, prepared by
> Ernest Tile, on p. 121.

> NOTE II.—Grass court tennis and croquet are
> equally fruitful fields for the Natural (or Natural-
> ist's) Hampette.
>
> See *Gardens for Gamesmen*, or *When to be Fond of
> Flowers* (15*s*.). To give verisimilitude to your
> natural history asides on the field of golf, or polo,
> or cricket, any good nature lover's booklet is

recommended.   O. Agnes Bartlett's *Moth's Way and Bee's Wayfaring* is a prettily illustrated general account.

NOTE III.—Against some players it is more irritating to point out any minute little grub and say, " Who would think, from its appearance now, that that little fellow will one day turn into a Peacock Blue! "

VII
GAME BY GAME

> " All ob one swallow am too much big swallow."
> *Up at Odoreida's.*

GOLF

IF I HAVE not said more about golf gamesmanship
it is because I am afraid of saying too much.   The
whole subject would make a volume in itself.   It is a
book which I feel should be the work of a younger
man.   Yet the fact remains that there are many
gamesmen who are not golfers.   Indeed, many good
steady gamesmen, knowing that golf is to me " the
gamesgame of gamesgames ", have started their
gamesplay of rackets or squash or whatever it may be
by saying to me " I'm afraid I don't play golf.   Do
you know, I've never been able to see the point of
it? "

My counter to this simple gambit has always been
to say : " No—it is, of course, a game of *pure* skill.   It
is the best game because no shot one plays can ever
be quite the same as any other shot.   Luck scarcely
enters into it, all one wants is fitness, a good eye, a
good nerve and a natural aptitude for games.   That's
why I like it."

The truth is, of course, that fitness counts for less in golf than in any other game, luck enters into every minute of the contest, and all play is purely incidental to, and conditioned by, gamesmanship.

To a young man about to undertake the teaching of our science in its special application to golf, I would stress the fact that he must make the student realise the extreme importance of Advicemanship, Bad Luck Play, with special attention to Commiseration, Luncheonship and, of course, the Secondary Hamper.

Then, when the student has properly mastered what I have nicknamed (and somehow the nickname has stuck!) " Four-up Friendliness ", and when— but not before—he is *really familiar* with, say, *ten* of the basic ways of walking off the tee after the drive with, or not with, the opponent—*then* go straight, say, to Caddie Play—but *don't* learn caddie management *or try to learn any other* secondary ploy, until the primary ploys have been mastered.

Then, for part two—the secondaries can be approached.   I suggest that their importance should be emphasised in this order :

1. *Splitting.*

In the foursome or four-ball game, this, quite simply, is the art of fomenting distrust between your two opponents.   And do not let the student forget, in the maze of details, that the basis of Split Play is to make friends with your opponent A, and in that same

process undermine his carefully assumed friendship—
so easily liable to strain—with his partner, your
opponent B, in order that, after the first bad shot
by B, the thought " Poor you! " may be clearly
implied by a glance from you, a shrug of the shoulders
or the whistling of two notes as recommended by
Gale (descending minor third).

NOTE.—Attention to detail is important
here, and may lead to results of even wider
value. It is possible to weaken your opponent's
attack even in a straightforward single, if you
can show sufficient parallelism of tastes and
interests. Groundwork includes the prelimin-
ary hunting out of the pursuits or hobbies
most favoured by the opponent to whom you
want to reveal the possession of those common
interests which may well be, you will wish him
to feel, the basis of a lasting friendship. And—
one tip—DON'T RUSH. Slow and steady wins this
race. Or, as I always tell them: " Keep off
Tintoretto till the tenth! " [1]

---

[1] R. Smart had a passion for Tintoretto so intense, that if an
opponent admitted to a similar interest in his paintings, Smart could
scarcely ever bring himself to beat him. On one occasion, however,
my friend G. Odoreida had an unfortunate experience. His match
with Smart was of supreme importance. He had practised for it by
an intensive three-weeks' study not only of Tintoretto but also of
Trienti, Tintoretto's celebrated pupil. He paid a flying visit to the
Mauritshuis, where there was a recent Tintoretto acquisition. At
the first hole, Odoreida plunged straight into the subject, not without genuine enthusiasm. But when, in consequence of this, he found
himself four up at the ninth hole, he made his first mistake. He
corrected Smart on a point of Tintoretto scholarship. Smart,
furious, fought back and beat him at the twentieth hole.

In the forefront, then, of secondary ploys, remember: Study the interests and tastes of your opponent. For

THE GOOD GAMESMAN IS THE GOOD FRIEND

2. *Caddie Play.*

The old rule still holds, " Be nice to your caddie and the game will be nice to you ". Demonstrate, always, that caddies instinctively like you and respect you more than they respect or even notice your opponent. Play to the caddie. Ask his advice. Create a pleasant caddie-liaison, and, when you whisperingly ask your opponent, in the neighbourhood of the sixteenth hole, what he proposes to offer as a tip, let your reply to his suggestion be: " What—do you mean two shillings as a *total tip*? Oh, I think we ought to give a little more than that." For remember that

THE GOOD GAMESMAN IS GENEROUS

NOTE.—Though this small ploy may work well against a diffident man playing on a strange course, it is sometimes advisable to say: " Oh, I don't think we ought to give them as much as that, you know. Members don't like it, you know. Do you remember when that Argentine Film Company was down here, flinging their money about? I'm not sure they weren't asked to leave the club. Of course, I see the Committee's point, in a way . . ." For remember that

THE GOOD GAMESMAN IS THE GOOD CLUBMAN

An Isolated Instance.

While these papers were still in the proof stage I was beaten in a certain golf match. I have not time to discuss the matter in full. I do not even know whether it comes in the province of gamesmanship. The incident was absurdly simple—almost comic. At the first hole, my opponent, D. Low, of Golders Green, drove into the edge of the rough. On reaching his ball, before playing it he picked it up and placed it in the fairway, saying, " I always do that. Do you mind? " Thinking that he intended not to play the hole at all—that his intention was perhaps to accompany me largely as a spectator—I laughed heartily, said, " Of course not," and settled down to a practice knockabout. Imagine my amazement when he proceeded thenceforward to play seriously and without further infringement. In my own mind the game was null and void from the beginning. But that did not prevent Low from presuming, indeed from saying, that he had in fact won.

Is this gamesmanhip? And if so, what is the counter?

Simpson's Statue.

I have been asked to give an exact explanation of a phrase used by many young gamesmen who do not, I fancy, properly know the meaning of the term, much less its origin.

FIG. 10.
Simpson's
Statue: the
billiards position.

I refer to the phrase " Simpson's Statue ", a simple gambit often used in croquet or snooker, but as it has its origin in golf, I place it here. R. Simpson had the idea of standing in the " wrong place " while his opponent was playing his shot—beyond the line of the putt in golf (or the pot in billiards). Or in the " wicket-keeper's position " during a golf shot off the fairway (or, in bowls, simply standing in the way). Having elicited a remonstrance, Simpson then proceeded, before every subsequent shot, not only in that game but in all subsequent matches against the same opponent, to remember that he was in the wrong position more or less at the last moment, leap into the correct position with exaggerated agility, and stand rigidly still with head bowed. (See Figs. 10 and 11.) Simpson, the originator of this ploy, used sometimes to increase its irritating effect by resting his club or cue head downwards on his boot, facetiously, in the " reversed arms " position. A simple but good

79

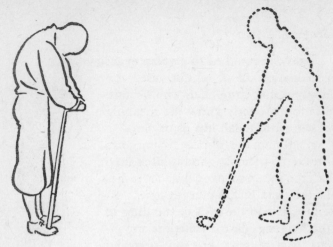

FIG. 11.—Advanced Simpson's Statue: the golf position, with "reversed arms" irritant (see p. 79).

gambit. And remember, to make it effective, repeat it again and again and again.

BILLIARDS AND SNOOKER

Although the close proximity of the players makes the billiard table almost as important to gamesmen as the golf-course, I have little to add to the much we have learned from this game. If snooker is inextricably bound up with gamesmanship, billiards is no less important. The ardent snooker gamesman plays billiards in order that he can say that " billiards is his real game ". There are the long periods, at billiards, during which no score is made. Its ·

ancient history, and dignified aroma of cigars and professional markers, adapt the game perfectly to this purpose. It is useful for the snooker gamesman to be in a position constantly to remind his snooker opponent that " billiards is *the* game ", also, that " billiards is the best practice for snooker ", and that he " will never improve his potting game until he has mastered the half-ball in-off at billiards ".

Snooker-player's Drivel.

I strongly recommend Rushington's one-and-sixpenny brochure on *Snooker-talk Without Tears.* This booklet contains full vocabularies of the drivellingly facetious language which has been found to be equally suitable to billiards and snooker, including a phonetic representation of such sounds as the imitation of the drawing of a cork, for use whenever the opponent's ball goes into the pocket. This is a most useful ploy against good billiard players of the older generation, who believe in correct manners and meticulous etiquette in the billiard room. I often saw Rushington at work in the good old days before the war. His masterpiece, I always thought, was never to say " five ", " eight ", etc., after scoring five, or eight, etc., but always " five skins ", " eight skins ", etc.

Remind students, here, that

THE GAMESMAN IS FAMOUS FOR HIS SENSE OF FUN

Unlike golf and billiards, squash is very far from being a gamesman's paradise. Most of the gamesman's work must be done beforehand, in the dressing-room or at the luncheon table. There is far too much ordinary play in this game, with all its dangers of physical distress, so fatal to the well-timed thrust of the gamesman. To counteract this disadvantage I always bring with me an old and even slightly punctured ball which I refer to as the " new, specially slow ball, recently authorised "; and I add that it is in general use now because " otherwise the rallies would never end ". If losing, stress inferiority of squash to rackets, which, in turn, of course, is so inferior to tennis. Thus, the sequence of talk runs as follows: " I was playing tennis at Lord's yesterday. This game's all right, but you know, after tennis, squash seems—well—you do feel rather like a squirrel running about in a cage, don't you? "

BRIDGE AND POKER

Miss Violet Watkins—name of ill-omen in gamesmanship circles on the Welsh border—has said that " Gamesmanship can play little part in bridge and poker, which are themselves games of bluff ".

The association of the word " bluff " with gamesmanship does small service to the art. True, there is a difficulty with poker. There are those who believe that the sole duty of the poker games-

man is to build up his reputation for impene-
trability and toughness by suggesting that he last
played poker by the light of a moon made more
brilliant by the snows of the Yukon, and that his
opponents were two white slave traffickers, a ticket-
of-leave man and a deserter from the Foreign Legion.
To me this is ridiculously far-fetched, but I do believe that a trace of American accent—West Coast—
casts a small shadow of apprehension over the minds
of English players.

Bridge, up to 1935, was virgin ground for the
gamesman, but every month—owing largely I believe to the splendid work of Meynell—new areas of
the game are being brought within his field. I will
name one or two of the principal *foci of research*, in the
new but growing world of bridgemanship.

1. *Intimidation.*

We are working now on methods by which the
gamesman can best suggest that he usually moves in
bridge circles far more advanced than the one in
which he is playing at the moment. This is sometimes difficult for the mediocre player, but a primary
gamescover of his more obvious mistakes is the frank
statement, with apologies, that the rough and ready
methods of this ordinary kind of bridge, played as it
is for amusingly low stakes, are constantly putting
him off. " Idiotic. I was thinking I was playing
duplicate." Refer to the " damnably complicated
techniques" with which matchplay is hedged around.

During the post-mortem period after each hand, give advice *to your opponents* immediately, before anyone else has spoken about the general run of the play. Tell the opponent on your left that " you saw her signalling with her third discard ". At first she will not realise that you are speaking to her, then she will not know what you are talking about, and will almost certainly agree. Invent " infringements " committed by your opponents in bidding, tell them that " it's quite all right—doesn't matter—but in a *match* it would be up to me to ask you to be silent for three rounds. Then if your partner redoubles, my original bid resumes its validity." Refer frequently to authorities. Mention the Portland Club and say " I expect you've only got the 1939 edition of the rules. Would you care to see the new thing I've got here? ' For Members only '? " Never say " It doesn't matter in the least what you throw away because I am leading this card at random anyhow." Refer to some formula in the *Silver Book of End-Play Squeezes*.

It is usual, as part of intimidation play, to *invent a convention* (if playing with a fellow-gamesman as partner). Explain the convention to your opponents, of course, e.g.:

GAMESMAN: Forcing two and Blackwood's, part-
      ner? Right? And Gardiner's as well?
      O.K.
LAYMAN: What's Gardiner's?
GAMESMAN: Gardiner's—oh, simply this. Some-

times comes in useful. If *you* call seven
diamonds *or* seven clubs and then one of us
doubles without having previously called
no trumps, then the doubler is telling his
partner, really, that in his hand are the
seven to Queen, *inclusive*, of the next highest
suit.

LAYMAN: I think I see. . . .

GAMESMAN: The situation doesn't arise very often,
as a matter of fact.

The fact that the situation does not arise more
often than once in fifty years prevents any possible
misunderstanding with your partner.

This phase of Intimidation Play is often called
" Conventionist " or " Conventionistical ".

2. *Two Simple Bridge Exercises for Beginners.*

(a) *The Deal.* Better than ten books on the theory
of bridge are the ten minutes a day spent in practising
how to deal. A startingly practised-looking deal has
a hypnotic effect on opponents, and many's the time
E. Hooper has won the rubber by his " spiral whirl "
type of dealing. A good deal of medical argument
has revolved round this subject. " Hooper's deal "
is actually said to have a pulverising effect on the
Balakieff layer of the cortex. Myself, I take this
cum grano salis.

(b) *Meynell's mis-deal.* This is, in essence, the
counter-game to intimidation play. Against a pair
of opponents who know each other's game very well

indeed, who have played together for years, and who
pride themselves on the mechanical and unhesitating
accuracy of their bidding, it is sometimes a good
thing to make a mis-deal deliberately (so that your
partner has fourteen and yourself twelve, say; or
the disparity may be even greater—see Fig. 12).
Then pick up the cards and begin a wild and irrational bidding sequence. This will end, of course,
in a double from E or W. As you begin to play the
hand, discover the discrepancy in cards. The hand
is then, of course, a wash-out. Your opponents will
(*a*) be made to look foolish, (*b*) be annoyed at missing
an easy double, (*c*) be unable to form a working
judgment of your bidding form.

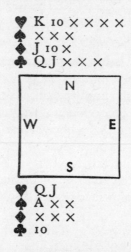

FIG. 12. Bridge hand. Distribution after typical Meynell mis-deal.

3. *Split Bridge*.

The old splitting game in golf foursomes has already been described (see p. 75). Of late years— it is, in fact, the most recent development in bridge— we have seen the adaptation of splitting, and the re-shaping of it, for the junior game.

The art of splitting, in bridge, is, quite simply, the art of sowing discord between your two opponents (East and West).

There is only one rule: BEGIN EARLY.

The first time the gamesman (South) makes his contract, the situation must be developed as follows:

GAMESMAN (South): Yes, just got the three. But I was rather lucky (*lowering voice to a clear whisper as he speaks to East*) . . . as a matter of fact your heart lead suited me rather well. I think . . . perhaps . . . if you'd led . . . well, almost anything else. . . .

Ten to one West will seize this first opportunity of criticising his partner and agree with Gamesman's polite implications of error. The seed of disagreement is sown. (Particularly if East had in fact led a heart correctly, or had not led one at all.) At the same time the gamesman's motto MODESTY AND SPORTMANSHIP is finely upheld. It is never his skill, but " an unlucky slip by his opponent ", which wins the trick.

The principal lawn tennis ploys have already been discussed (see Index). I should like to add here one word more of general advice. If there is one thing I hate to see on the lawn tennis court, it is sloppy gamesmanship. And much more attention should be paid, I think particularly, to the following evolutions:

(1) How to pass opponent when changing ends, particularly the choice of the right moment to stand elaborately aside in order to allow your female opponent, in a mixed doubles, to come through first: and equally when to allow her the minimum room for getting by.

(2) When to make a great show of encouraging your partner, and say " Good SHOT ", whenever she gets the ball back over the net.

(3) How to apologise for lobbing into the sun.

(4) When to get the scoring wrong (always, of course, in your opponent's favour).

NOTE.—I have already referred (p. 15) to Farjeon's use of asymmetrical lengths, slopes and grass surfaces of his lawn tennis court at Forest Hill. It has been said of Farjeon that he raised lawn tennis to the status of a Home Game. It was after association with Farjeon that I began that development of Home Croquet which has placed it so far ahead of the championship game. Major West, of Gamesman Accessories Ltd., where Gamesman Accessories may be obtained, has constructed an artificial hawthorn tree for asymmetrical insertion into the normal croquet lawn. Illustrated below (Fig. 13) is Major West's "Baskerville" lawn tennis lawn-marker for home courts. This reliable machine imparts the standard "3″ wave" to lines even on the most level lawns.

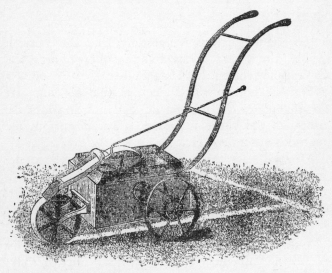

FIG. 13. The Baskerville Lawn Tennis-Marker for imparting asymmetry to home courts (see text).

HOME GAMES

There are a variety of odd local games, and games developed in the home—"roof-game", "tishy-toshy", etc. Unorthodox games, like billiards fives, or *boule*—the game of bowls played with metal balls.

All these need careful gamesmanship, and are admirably adapted to a wide variety of ploys.

The player on the home court stands at a tremendous advantage, specially if he has invented the rules of the game. He must rub this advantage in by every method at his command.

Terminologics.

To counteract any suggestions that the game is " silly ", he should create an atmosphere of historical importance round it. He should suggest its universality, the honour in which it is held abroad. He should enlarge on the ancient pageantry in which the origin of the game is vested, speak of curious old methods of scoring, etc.

Meynell uses the word " terminologics " to describe the very complete language we have built round the game of *boule* (which in our game consists of rolling old bits of brass into a cracked gutter).

NOTE TO TEACHERS.—It is most important that the student should develop methods of his own. Encourage originality. But perhaps teachers may be helped by seeing this specimen of a " correspondence " which " passed " between Meynell and myself. This we incorporated in a privately printed pamphlet *English Boule* which we leave about in the bath-rooms, etc., of the boule court house. The specimen may suggest, at any rate, a general approach.

Dear Meynell,

I forgot, when I was writing to advise you on the financial matter, to say that I had checked up on the point you mentioned, and it is not uninteresting to note that the expression *bowels* (i.e., boules) *of compassion* " first used in 1374 " has no connection with the ancient etiquette, recently revived as we know, according to which the gouttie-étranger (the gutstranger, or guest player new to the boule " carpet ") is supposed to allow his host to win the " bully-up ", or first rubber sequence. The term, of course, acquired its modern use much later in connection with the boule game which the Duke of Rutland played for a wager against Henry, son of Shakespeare's " old Gaunt, time-honoured Lancaster " at Hove Castle in 1381, beating him on the last throw with a half-pansy, and dubbing his victim " Bouling-broke ", an amusing nickname which, spoken in jest, became as we know the patronymic of the Dukes of Lancaster.

Yours,

" *My Man Over the Hill.*"

There is an excellent alternative to the development of a private game in your own home. That is to do the same thing in a house belonging to someone else. This is not only inconvenient to the real owner of the house; it places you in the fine games-position of " playing on a strange court ".

J. Strachey has invented a form of indoor hockey which is played with the pointed end of an ordinary walking-stick as the club. As a game it is feebleness itself. But Strachey uses an interesting gameoplay in its execution.

The game is played in an old shed, five to fourteen a side. Early in the game Strachey says:

> "Hi—whoa!—Look everybody. Wait a minute, wait a minute. Wait a minute, everybody. We mustn't lift our sticks above the knee, must we. Or else one of us will get the most awful cut. Right."

He then proceeds, quite deliberately, to lay about him to right and left so that nobody can come near him. Through this method he has amassed an amazing sequence of wins to his credit.

CHESS

The prime object of gamesmanship in chess must always be, at whatever sacrifice, to build up your reputation. In our small chess community in Marylebone it would be mock modesty on my part to deny that I have built up for myself a considerable name without ever actually having won a single game.

Even the best players are sometimes beaten, and that is precisely what happens to me. Yet it is always possible to make it appear that you have lost your game *for the game's sake*.

"*Regardez la Dame*" Play.

This is done by affecting anxiety over the wiseness of your opponent's move. An occasional " Are you sure you meant that? " or " Your castle won't like that in six moves' time " works wonders.

By arrangement with another gamesman I have made an extraordinary effect on certain of our Marylebone Chess Club Rambles by appearing to engage him in a contest without board. In the middle of a country lane I call out to him " P to Q3 ", then a quarter of an hour later he calls back to me " Q to QB5 "; and so on. " Moves ", of course, can be invented arbitrarily.

> JUNIOR MEMBER: I can't think how you do it.
> SELF: Do what?
> JUNIOR MEMBER: Play chess without the pieces. Do you have a *picture* of the board in your brain . . . or what is it?
> SELF: Oh, you mean our little game? I am actually up at the moment. Oh, you mean how do we do it? Oh, I've always been able to " see " the board in that way, ever since I can remember.

Potter's Opening.

This is supposed, now, to be the name of an effective opening, simple to play and easy to remember, which I have invented for use against a more experienced player who is absolutely certain to win. It consists of making three moves at random and then resigning. The dialogue runs as follows:

FIG. 14. Potter's opening. (1) KP–K4 : KP–K4.
(2) B–Q B4 : B–Q B4.
(3) Kt–B3 : Kt–B3.
(4) White resigns.

SELF: Good. Excellent. (*Opponent has just made his third move. See Fig. 14*). I must resign, of course.

OPPONENT: Resign?

SELF: Well . . . you're bound to take my Bishop after sixteen moves, unless . . . unless . . . And even then I lose my castle three moves later.

OPPONENT: Oh, yes.

SELF: Unless you sacrifice there, which, of course, you wouldn't.

OPPONENT: No.

SELF: Nice game.

OPPONENT: Yes.

SELF: Pretty situation . . . very pretty situation. Do you mind if I take a note of it? The *Chess News* usually publishes any stuff I send them.

It is no exaggeration to say that this gambit, boldly carried out against the expert, heightens the reputation of the gamesman more effectively than the most courageous attempt to fight a losing battle.

Chess and Parentship, or Gamesplay against Children.

Many of the regular rules have to be adapted, with a tender hand, I hope and trust, when one exercises gamesmanship against the young. E.g., much use can be made of the fact that *children cannot remember their own infancy* (Grotto's Law). For instance, if beaten by my son at chess, I tell him (i) that I have only just taken it up, and (ii) that " my first recollection of him was of a tiny figure sitting astride a wall, swinging his legs and playing chess with his minute friend Avrion. Neither of them can have been more than five at the time. How glad I am that I encouraged him to take it up."

Basic Chess Play.

" Sitzfleisch." I have the greatest pleasure in assigning priority to F. V. Morley who first described this primary chessmanship gambit (see Morley, F. V., *My One Contribution to Chess*, Faber and Faber, 1947). Morley's wording is as follows:

> Sitzfleisch: a term used in chess to indicate

winning by use of the glutei muscles—the habit of remaining stolid in one's seat hour by hour, making moves that are sound but uninspired, until one's opponent blunders through boredom.

Johnsonian Capture.

The name of Miss C. Johnson will always be associated primarily with certain specialised techniques or styles, recommended, of course, for women only, in the method of capturing pieces. It is, in essence, Differentiated Intimidation play. Playing against men, she has had extraordinary success by soundlessly and delicately removing her opponent's piece before quietly placing her own piece on the square. But against women, particularly nervous women, she bangs down her own piece with great force on the occupied square, so that her opponent's piece is, of course, sent sprawling over the board.

By the way, it is not true to say that Miss C. Johnson, who for some years now has been giving lessons in the " Johnsonian Capture ", is the first P.G.W.A.[1] Readers will remember the unfortunate case of Miss J. Wethered, whose name in golf might now be forgotten were it not for the famous case in which she was deemed to have infringed on her professional gameswoman status by a series of matches, much too long to pass unnoticed, which were later proved, beyond possible doubt, to have been genuinely friendly.

[1] Member of the Professional Gameswomen's Association.

DARTS AND SHOVE-HALFPENNY

Basic play in these games must always be a variation of the Primary Hamper. Question your darts opponent closely on the exact area of the dart where he deems it wisest to exert maximum thumb-and-finger pressure. Continue to ask if he will be so kind as to demonstrate for you the precise position of the hand in relation to the head at the moment when the dart is released. In the case of shove-halfpenny, hold up game continually by asking your opponent if he " will touch with the end of a match the area of the ball of the thumb which should be regarded as the target-of-impact between skin and receiving edge of disc of ' halfpenny ' ".

In playing these games on home boards, where you might be presumed to have an advantage, keep talking about " How you prefer old pub boards . . . nothing like genuine pub boards. . . ."

CRICKET

If there is one thing more than another which makes me regret those pressing requests of my friends which forced me to " rush into print " with this volume, it is the fact that the huge subject of Cricket must remain a blank in this edition of my work. G.R.C.(C) (or, to give it its full, rather ponderous, title, Gamesmanship Research Council, Cricket Division) has been in existence scarcely five years. A devoted band of workers have spent their spare time in its service for no other reward than a nominal expenses account, an entertainment allowance, and the nominal use of the Council's cars and petrol. It will be remembered that after five researchers had found 8,400 instances of gamesmanship in a match at Hove, reduced by rain to a bare one and a half days' play, between Sussex and Derbyshire, the investigation was completely re-organised, following the resignation of the then Chairman, Sir William (now Lord) Tile, the brother of E. Tile, the sportsman. This meant, virtually, the scrapping of two years' work, when the researchers were given their new briefing, and sent out all over again in an effort to discover some game, or some act in some game, of cricket, in which gamesmanship was *not* involved.

But results are beginning to come in now. Four instances have been recorded from Surrey alone. By 1949 there should be something in print. Till then, good luck to the G.R.C.(C), and good hunting. The chapter on " Spectatorship ", or the " art of winning the watching ", as it has been called, is to be, I am glad to say, in the able hands of Colonel Debenham.

NOTE.—Historians of gamesmanship often ask the following question: " It is said that there is some mystery about the connection between cricket and G. Odoreida, the celebrated gamesman. What is it? "

The answer is simple. There is no mystery,

for the facts are known. Odoreida did well in his early cricketing days as a spectator, particularly at Old Trafford. He was the first to enclose the Complete Records of Cricket in the cover of Bradshaw's Railway Guide, so that when, in order to win an argument, he was "recalling", say, Verity's bowling average of 1931 he was able to achieve accuracy up to two places of decimals, while to the admiring onlookers it seemed that he was casually verifying the time of a train.

But this spectatorship of Odoreida's soon had too many imitators: and after he took to the game itself, he was never really successful. When it came to such straightforward irritation gambits as the movements of sightscreens, Odoreida found that the ordinary average cricketer could outgame him every time. Some of the devices he fell back upon were not very happily chosen. He spent an entire season acquiring absolute ambidexterity as a batsman. Coming in eighth wicket down, he was able to irritate an already wearied field by playing alternate balls left- and right-handed, forcing the fielders to change position after each delivery. As a bowler (according to F. Meynell, quoting H. Farjeon), his habit was to shout "no ball", imitating the accent and voice of the umpire, as the ball left his hand. This gambit got him an occasional wicket, but it was frowned upon by the older generation of gamesmen.

VIII
LOST GAME PLAY

"... for the game is one of a series,
And a fractional loser thou."

THE value of gamesmanship as a training for the British citizen, and for young people in particular, is shown not only in the special qualities it enhances among those who habitually find themselves on the losing side. If it is true that the typical Britisher never knows when he has lost, it is true of the typical gamesman that his opponent never knows when he has won.

The true gamesman knows that the game is never at an end. Game-set-match is not enough. The winner must win the winning. And the good gamesman is never known to lose, even if he has lost.

To take one example. Tony Gillies was no snooker player, and no golfer either. But he had this gift—of turning defeat into something very near complete victory. If the match was " serious "— Club event or handicap—he would paint himself as the Abe Mitchell of club golf, who had won everything but the cup. He would bring out astonishing details of unpopular members who had won the event, and refer to their dull struggles, their ant-like methods of overcoming difficulties . . . characters without temperament, and without interest.

Conversely, of course, if the match he lost had been " only a friendly ", he would say, " I don't think I've won a *friendly* match this year. There is some devilish twist in my character which condemns me only to win a match if it is really important. Sheer blind desperation, I suppose."

Bookmanism.

This is the place to mention the basic Lost Game Play originated, I believe, by Rupert Duff, of water-polo fame. And I should like to say here that I bear no grudge against the followers of the Oxford Group for their punning use of the term " Buchmanite " transliterated from my own " Bookmanite ", " Book-manism ", etc. But let me remind readers that the term BOOKMANISM, in its original sense, bore no reference to gamesmanship in religion, but was used to cover that small, highly specialised, but very valuable ploy in the Lost Game, which includes the possession of books on the game, and the knowledge of the right moment to recommend them, and to lend them.

This is more effective even than the suggestion that your opponent, " now that he is doing so well ", should " have a couple of lessons from the pro (and mind you stick to what he says) ". In at least three respects it is more likely to undermine his game.

" Take my tip," you say to him, " and study this little book by Z. It's worth a dozen practice games. Don't take another practice shot till you've mastered the first twelve chapters. Then make up your mind to put into execution what you've learnt. Even if it means losing a game or two."

Use of Bookmanism in Opponent's Putt-Play.

I am supposed to be something of a fanatic in the use of Bookmanism where Golf is concerned. I have collected a small library of books on the different aspects of the game. The book I select for lending is determined when I have decided which aspect of my winning opponent's play it is most advisable to undermine. But, in general, all " golfgamesers " are agreed that " the putt is the thing to go for ". " ANALYSE YOUR OPPONENT'S PUTTING " is the Golden Rule. Ask him what muscles he brings into play, and from what part of the body the " sequence of muscular response " begins. To deal · with opponents who say that they " aren't aware of using any muscles in particular ", O.G.A. are issuing the accompanying diagram-leaflet, with instructions on how to present it. (See opposite.)

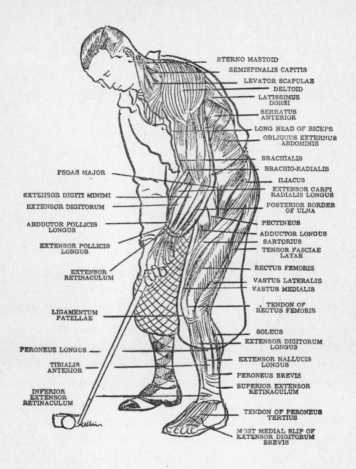

STERNO MASTOID

SEMISPINALIS CAPITIS

LEVATOR SCAPULAE

DELTOID

LATISSIMUS DORSI

SERRATUS ANTERIOR

LONG HEAD OF BICEPS

OBLIQUUS EXTERNUS ABDOMINIS

BRACHIALIS

BRACHIO-RADIALIS

ILIACUS

EXTENSOR CARPI RADIALIS LONGUS

POSTERIOR BORDER OF ULNA

PECTINEUS

ADDUCTOR LONGUS

SARTORIUS

TENSOR FASCIAE LATAE

RECTUS FEMORIS

VASTUS LATERALIS

VASTUS MEDIALIS

TENDON OF RECTUS FEMORIS

SOLEUS

EXTENSOR DIGITORUM LONGUS

EXTENSOR HALLUCIS LONGUS

PERONEUS BREVIS

SUPERIOR EXTENSOR RETINACULUM

TENDON OF PERONEUS TERTIUS

MOST MEDIAL SLIP OF EXTENSOR DIGITORUM BREVIS

PSOAS MAJOR

EXTENSOR DIGITI MINIMI

EXTENSOR DIGITORUM

ABDUCTOR POLLICIS LONGUS

EXTENSOR POLLICIS LONGUS

EXTENSOR RETINACULUM

LIGAMENTUM PATELLAE

PERONEUS LONGUS

TIBIALIS ANTERIOR

INFERIOR EXTENSOR RETINACULUM

FIG. 15.—IMPORTANT: This illustration, taken from p. 472 of Weil's *Primer of Putting*, should not be shown to opponent until the third week.

GAMESMANIANA

RANDOM JOTTINGS OF AN OLD GAMESMAN

by

" Wayfarer "

". . . And the gamesman's gone from the ghyll."

When the first crocus breaks cover, and the branches of the still-bare trees are peopled once more with sound as the birds begin to practise their spring song, that is the time when the hearts of gamesmen, young and old, stir at the thoughts of triumphs to come. They stir in another way, too, when the last leaf falls and the branches grow silent—stir with memories, then, of a season past, remembrance echoing with the small victories, the tiny conquests, recalling to their minds some grand old phrases of the gamesplay—" Loseman's Hamper ", or " the weak heart of Morteroy ", memories of the triumphs and failures of the gamesacre.

Which reminds me—by the way—that the Old
Gamesman's Association continues to grow. O.G.A.
or "the Ogres", as they are affectionately called,
meet twice a year to deliver judgment on their
validity, as a body, and to describe advances in
technique. Welcome, also, to the new Ogre tie—
and what a sensible notion it was to make the colours
and pattern of this special tie precisely the same as
that worn by the I. Zingaris! This has the triple
advantage of (1) doing away with the need of design-
ing a special tie, (2) allowing the gamesman to be
mistaken for one who has the very exclusive honour of
belonging to I.Z., and (3) irritating any genuine I.Z.
against whom the gamesman happens to be playing.

A QUEER MATCH

No, the O.G.s don't take themselves too seriously.
And what a good thing that is! I had the good
fortune to be present at the celebrated badminton
match between G. Odoreida and the Yugo-Slav
champion Bzo in the West Regional Finals—one of
the longest games I have ever watched. Both were
poor players. Both were at the height of their
gamesmanship powers. The match started a good
hour before the game began. Odoreida kept Bzo's

taxi waiting twelve minutes and then was short of change when the time came for payment. But the younger player succeeded in exacting his share and came out of it a shilling to the good, only to find himself one rum and orange to the bad on the drink exchange before their sandwich lunch. In the changing-room Bzo prettily pleaded a cut on the palm of his right hand, which he had swathed elaborately in a special grip-improving elastoplast earlier in the morning. Odoreida Frith-Morteroyed in reply, displaying his little finger, the top joint of which was missing. " Jet plane," he said. " The skin has just healed." This was dangerous, for many of us knew that the accident happened thirty-five years ago, when Odoreida caught his finger in the chain of a toy tricycle.

The game itself started with some efficient crowd play. Odoreida opened by exchanging jokes with the umpire, and Bzo countered by patting the head of the shuttlecock boy and comically pretending to be hurt when a return from Odoreida hit him gently in the middle of the chest. Odoreida drew level by smashing into the net on purpose, after the umpire had (quite correctly) given a line-cock decision in his favour. The applause had hardly died down when Bzo jumped into the lead again. Odoreida had made the mistake of achieving his first hard shot of the game, and Bzo made no attempt to reach it but stood stock still, shaking his head from side to side in whimsical respect, and sporting acknowledgment of his opponent's skill. Odoreida did well soon after this by discovering a " sprung string " in his racquet and asking with delightful informality whether " anyone had got another bat " as he had not got a spare. This double thrust shook Bzo for a few points, but he soon pulled himself together by asking a spectator " not to wave his programme about " as it was " bang in his opponent's line of sight ". Bzo seemed in full spate. Odoreida, now badly rattled, fought back well with a couple of broken shoe-laces and a request for a lump of sugar. Thus gambit after gambit was tried, and each in turn was effectively countered. After an hour's play they were still on the first game and the score was deuce for the sixtieth time, when suddenly Bzo came up to the net and spoke as follows:

" Let's " (or " Why not let's ") " drop gamesmanship and just play? "

Odoreida assented and the game was then *played*, to the end. It had, of course, lost all interest to the more understanding spectators, who were puzzled, to say the least, although a small group applauded.

At the same time, I do not feel we should blame them too heavily. For

GAMESMANSHIP CAN BE TAKEN TOO SERIOUSLY

GAMESMANSHIP
AND LIFE

As I was endeavouring to think of a phrase which would express some of our deeper feelings on the subject of this queer Science of ours, the heading was supplied, as if by chance, in a way which was as unexpected as it was kind. When my wife brought me my post I knew, from the superscription, whence the letter came. "My dear," I said, "here is something from the Dean of Southport." He had written to ask me to come along and chat to his lads up there on the theme of Gamesmanship and Life. It is certainly amazing—and I was favourably astonished—to see the interest expressed by Young People of all denominations in my small theories.

I noticed how readily gamesmanship appealed to the young when I watched my own two lads picking it up with increasing aptitude, and using it, too, in boyhood games of ping-pong and lawn tennis, croquet and chess. And how pleased we were when, sometimes, their little efforts succeeded against us.[1]

I think it is the fact that sportsmanship and chivalry are the so frequently repeated watchwords

[1] *v.* "Counter-Gamesmanship, Parents and ", p. 95.

of gamesmanship, which makes it appeal so strongly to young persons, and to much older people also, like the Dean of Southport, who must have noticed the constant use we make of these phrases in our magazines and pamphlets.

I think my visit was a success. I know it was of benefit to myself. When I went up for my lecture—group-chat would describe it better—I soon had them smiling and asking questions. And I was glad to do even this small office towards the ensuring of that continuance of growth, that ever-widening circle, which will help us to look to the future, while we are remembering the past.

APPENDIX I

The Köninck Portrait of Dr. W. G. Grace

There are still certain points which need clearing up on the subject of the disputed portrait of the great doctor.

Fig. 16. The Köninck Portrait of W. G. Grace (see text).

The dust of controversy has settled, by now. Yet it is amusing to recall that fifty years ago the Köninck portrait of Grace was always reproduced as a proof that the famous beard was false. Grace certainly used his beard like a good gamesman, and no doubt this fact, and the obvious advantages of a large black beard, gave rise to the rumour. It was said that the join of the beard to the neck (N on the picture) was faked. Mr. Samuel Courtauld first came into prominence as an investigator of pictures by stepping forward to point out that at the mouth (M on the picture) the join was obviously natural.

The extraordinary success of Grace as a gamesman has led to an astounding crop of stories associated with his name. Half the cricket theorists in England have vied with each other in the invention of the unlikeliest tales.

The Gladstonian Theory.

Ridiculous theories were particularly rife in 1888 as to the " real identity " of the great doctor. The Köninck portrait usually figures largely in these discussions. If the cap in the portrait is supposed to show the colours of the Wanderers, why the monogram? And if the monogram shown is that of the Gloucester Colts, why the button on the top of the head? Microscopic examination has shown, too, that the shirt, instead of buttoning left over right, folds right over left. Was Grace a woman?

The theory that Grace was really Gladstone became, of course, the sporting sensation of the century. The doctrine is based on the " concealed meaning " of two words, the most important words spoken by Gladstone in the whole of his career, or at any rate, the words which *he seemed to wish the world to believe* the

most important. This was his asseveration, when he
first assumed the office of Prime Minister, that PACIFY
IRELAND was to be his mission. The theory is, of
course, that when Gladstone spoke of Ireland, he was
referring not to the famous country but to J. H.
Ireland, the Australian fast bowler.

The one man who knew the answer to the secret—
R. G. S. (" Flicker ") Wilson—kept his mouth—now
closed for ever—firmly shut during his lifetime. It is
certainly true that Gladstone, if he had in fact been
Grace, would have had more reason to fear the Ireland of the cricketing world, and indeed Gladstone's
suddenly assumed interest in Ireland is difficult to
explain. Gladstonians have gone to fantastic lengths
to read double meanings into the wordings of Gladstone's Home Rule Bills. They prove, to their own
conviction at any rate, that it was Home Rule for
England which was Gladstone's main concern, fore-
seeing as he undoubtedly did the menace of Australian
Test Match cricket.

But the whole theory breaks down, surely, on the
question of dates. Is it true that Grace was never
seen batting at Lord's during the Midlothian campaign? What is the value of the evidence of D. Bell
that his grandfather once " thought he heard Grace
laughing in the Long Room " during this period?
Again, J. H. Ireland was only twenty-six when Gladstone assumed office. His play had been reported in
The Times, but only three members of the M.C.C. had
seen him bowl, including Price. And it is I suppose
just conceivably possible that Gladstone did fre-

quently refer to "Price's Message", if by a simple transliteration references to Lord Rosebery can be shown to be references to Price.

But Grace or Gladstone, who cares? As any sportsman will say, here was some magnificent cricket played by a magnificent cricketer, who gave pleasure to the world, be his name what it may.

APPENDIX II

NOTE ON ETIQUETTE

IT IS EXTRAORDINARY how often, among gamesmen, the etiquette of gamesplay is instinctive, and there is little need, I am glad to say, to reduce etiquette to the formality of print.

There are two points, nevertheless, on which questions are sometimes asked. I append the official answers.

(*a*) When two gamesmen are playing together, it is usual for the senior gamesman to make the first move.

(*b*) When two or more gamesmen are playing against opponents *or with partners* who are not gamesmen, none of the gamesmen should make any reference to gamesmanship either directly or by using such phrases as "don't take any notice of what he says", "he's pulling your leg", etc.

APPENDIX III

Play Among Primitive Animals: the Limpet —Significance of " Fishy "—Cat and Mouse and the Study of *Ur* Gamesmanship—The Neolithic Gap—Some Unexplained Greek Vase Paintings —The Indecipherable " Prayer Sheets " Found in Londonderry—Persian Origin of the Phrase " Velvet Glove "—St. Augustine's Find—Chinese Emblem for " Playing a Losing Game "— Gift of " Tennis Balls " to Henry V—Gamesmanship and the Battle of Agincourt—Symbolism of the Pawns, in Chess—Renaissance—of what?—Boyhood of Francis Drake—Difference Between Machiavelli and Cervantes—Use of Latin Quotations—Rembrandt's first " Tam-o-Shanter " Self-Portrait Examined—The Nineteenth Century and After—After That—Dawn of Cricket—Dawn of Not Cricket—W. G. Grace's Beard: False or Genuine ?—Use of Linesmen in Wimbledon Lawn Tennis—End of the Era of Actual Play, in Games.

APPENDIX IV

DIET

I DO NOT favour any fads or frills where diet for gamesmanship is concerned. Eat what you please seems to be the Golden Rule. But in moderation. A sufficient breakfast, wholesome lunch—and there is no reason why it should not be palatable as well. "A little of what you fancy" at tea-time. And a well-balanced, well-cooked evening meal completes the scheme, and should satisfy the wants of the average gamesman. Fats are important and carbohydrates should not be neglected, provided that protein content is kept in mind. But always remember that the meal before play should not be too heavy, nor the meal afterwards too light.

APPENDIX V

THE *Gamesman's Handbook* (1949) is now in prepara-
tion and it is hoped to publish it at the beginning of
December 1948—not in order to take advantage of
any adventitious catch-sale at Christmas, but because the birthday of our popular treasurer falls in
that month.   It is hoped to make the volume a com-
bination of Wisden and Baedeker, with full accounts
of the principal clubs, hotels which cater for the
O.G.A., garages which will accept custom, etc., etc.

Here is an extract from the earliest of many interesting tables:

OPEN CHAMPIONSHIP.

1929	Miss E. Goodhart
1930	,,
1931	,,
1932	,,
1933	,,
1934	,,
1935	G. Odoreida

The professional side of gamesmanship will receive
full attention.   Extracts from an article by " V. V.":

> The low status of the amateur gamesman, in
> Great Britain, is a factor which we should never be
> allowed to forget.   In America it is difficult to tell the

pro from the amateur. In Britain, the feeble clothes and general appearance of the amateur single him out at once. We amateurs have to fight against the growing menace of young people who insist on playing their various games for the fun of the thing, treating it all as a great lark, and indulging rather too freely, if the truth were known, in pure play.

There is no doubt that a knowledge of the game itself sometimes helps the gamesman. But there is a growing tendency to carry this too far in some professional circles. An interesting point arose when Kinroyd of Hoylake, the local Professional Gamesmen's Association representative, holed the course in seventy-two, the standard scratch score. Had he or had he not lost his professional status? And, if so, what profession?

Record Games and Queer Incidents.

A selection from the Handbook List.

(8) In March 1929 G. Wert won the Isle of Purbeck Shield Knock-out Competition. In the six rounds played, he never holed out in less than ninety-two net. On presenting the prize, Lady Armory complimented him on his success in the face of wretched play and referred in her speech to the

" literally unadulterated " gamesmanship of the player.

(22) On eight separate occasions, all within a fortnight, playing in the same club, against the same group of opponents, J. Batt won his match, using the same gamesplay on each occasion (" I'm an awful fool, but I've had no food for twenty-four hours "). After one match, the loser actually sent him a present of butter.

(41) Captain E. Mawdesley Hill, in the autumn of 1938, won three successive matches against –. Johns of Forest Grove, in three successive weeks, by asking him, with great delicacy, *on each occasion*, whether he (–. Johns) was in financial difficulties and would he accept help. It is interesting to note that a fourth game was also lost when –. Johns realised not only that no kind of help was forthcoming, but that on the contrary Mawdesley Hill owed him for two lunches. –. Johns was too angry to control his game.

(182) *Distinguished Visitor Play.* J. Strachey made beautiful use of this gambit in a recent lawn tennis doubles " friendly " in which " Wayfarer " was concerned. The game was played at a time when Anglo- * * * * -ish relations were cordial, but delicately balanced. " To my surprise ", writes " Wayfarer ", " Strachey, asking if he could bring his own partner, astonished us by turning up with the * * * *-ish Ambassador. Before the game began Strachey took me

aside to ' explain the position '. He suggested that
the game should be played, ' for obvious reasons ',
without gamesmanship. On the whole (he tipped
me the wink) it would be no bad thing if the Ambassador (who was, of course, Strachey's partner)
ended up on the winning side. ' Someone on the
highest level ' had hinted as much to him.

" Pleased to comply, my partner and I obediently
lost the first set. Before the next set began, however,
Strachey let it slip out that he had been pulling our
leg, that it was not the * * * *-ish Ambassador at
all, but—and here it seemed to me that I recognised the
vaguely familiar face—one of the Oval Umpires who
in his spare time played lawn tennis as a member of
the East Kennington L.T.C. This silly trick angered
me, and my play in the second set was not improved
in consequence, particularly as we both drove hard
at the Oval man's body but, in our annoyance,
usually missed it. Two sets to Strachey.

" In the third set Strachey out-manoeuvred us
once more. He told us, finally, that in fact his
partner really was the * * * *-ish Ambassador, who,
indeed, he turned out to be. This, of course, completely upset us, the remembrance of our rude behaviour in Set II rendering us almost incapable of
returning the simplest ball. This gave Strachey the
third set and the match.

" The whole game, which was played on an
asphalt court, lasted exactly fifty-eight minutes."

NOTE.—J. Strachey writes: " I note that
' Wayfarer ' actually left the court under the

impression that the player in question *was* the ****-ish Ambassador. Be that as it may . . . has not our good 'Wayfarer' for once missed the point, or rather perhaps the principle *behind* the point, of this little incident? The real crux was the creation of doubt in the opponent's mind. In this case, for example, our opponents sometimes supposed themselves to be facing the ****-ish Ambassador and sometimes one of the Oval Umpires; not unnaturally they failed adequately to adjust their play. But that does not exclude the possibility that the fourth player in the set was the Ambassador of another power, or alternatively, of course, an Umpire, not of the Surrey C.C., but of an *entirely different* County Club."

We are glad to say that the *Gamesman's Handbook* will be, in its new edition, plentifully pictured with half-tone blocks and illustrations in photogravure. G. G. P.[1] and G.O.[2] have completed their survey by including the areas of West Riding and Lanarkshire. We reproduce two illustrations (Figs. 17 and 18) representing the results of their pooled researches.

[1] Gallup Poll, Gamesman's Division.
[2] Gamesmen's Mass Observation, usually shortened to Gass O. or G.O.

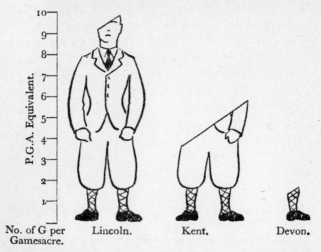

FIG. 17. Showing the distribution of Gamesmen's Associations in **three** typical English counties, to explain the zoning of OGA in relation to PGA.

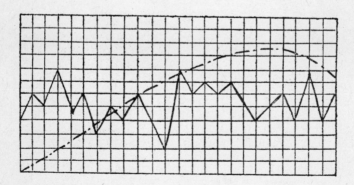

FIG. 18. Graph showing the relationship between Mean Bird Gamesmanship and Mean Game Birdmanship.

GLOSSARIAL INDEX

A

ADVICEMANSHIP, 44
" After All ", 70
Amateur gamesman, low status of, 116
Audience play, 30

B

Bad Luck Play, 75
Badminton, 105–107
Ballmanship, Better, 48
" Baskerville " Lawn Tennis-Marker, 89
Batt, J., 118
Bell, D., grandfather of, 112
Billiards, 34, 80–81; cue-chalking, 28; use of telephone, in, 35; when to give advice in, 44; use of Improved Primitive in, 60
Birdmanship, Game, 72, 120
Birkbeck College, traditional birthplace of Gamesmanship, 16
" Bohn's Tables ", i.e. Bohn's *Pause and the Distraction Factor Mathematically Considered, with Tables of Mean Optimum Time Lengths and an Appendix on Hesitations*, 21
Bookmanism, 101
Boule, 90–91
Bowls, use of luncheon interval in, 57
Bridge, contract, 82–87
Bzo, U., holder (1947) Yugo-Slav Gamesmanship Championship. His match with Odoreida, 105

C

Caddie Play, 77
Cardiac affections, minor, knowledge of, 40

entrants, in three successive years. Simpson, who owes his success, in still-ball games, to the constant repetition of one gambit (see p. 79), is sometimes described as the founder of the "Simpson School".
Drinkmanship and, 53; origin of Simpson's statue, 79
Sitzfleisch, 95
Snooker, 80–82; and audience play, 31, 34; counterpoint in, 35; fluke play, 46
Squash-rackets, 82; nose-blowing and, 59; leaking roof, used in, 61; and Ruggership, 69
"Splitting", in golf, 75; in bridge, 87
Sportsmanship, 27
Stakesmanship, 29
Strachey, Rt. Hon. J. played for Essex Colts, 1940; capped, 1941; quarter-finalist, 1942. His meteoric career in Gamesmanship has been described in *The Strachey I Grew to Know*, by "Wayfarer". Indoor hockey of, 91; and ****-ish Ambassador, 118
Sussexmanship, or the use and abuse of scenic beauty. (*Sussex*, name of Sussex, the county), 71

T

Tearle, Godfrey, and croquet, 33
Tennis, 32; ruggership, possibilities of, 69
Terminologics, 90
Tile, Ernest, graph of, 120
Tile, Lord, 98
Tipmanship, 77
Trains, railway, use of, 27, 44

U

Umpire, Play, 106; Oval, 119

W

Watson, Miss E., pioneer of Clothesmanship, 25
West, G., 117
Wethered, Miss J., and railway trains, 44
Winmanship, 43
Winner's heartiness, 54